Soul-Saving Women

Soul-Saving Women

Guerline Reid

XULON PRESS

Xulon Press
2301 Lucien Way #415
Maitland, FL 32751
407.339.4217

www.xulonpress.com

© 2022 by Guerline Reid

All rights reserved solely by the author. The author guarantees all contents are original and do not infringe upon the legal rights of any other person or work. No part of this book may be reproduced or transmitted in any form or by any means without written permission of the author. The views expressed in this book are not necessarily those of the publisher.

Due to the changing nature of the Internet, if there are any web addresses, links, or URLs included in this manuscript, these may have been altered and may no longer be accessible. The views and opinions shared in this book belong solely to the author and do not necessarily reflect those of the publisher. The publisher therefore disclaims responsibility for the views or opinions expressed within the work.

Unless otherwise indicated, Scripture quotations taken from the King James Version (KJV)—*public domain.*

This work was compiled through a research of many sources including the Bible, books, articles, and reference sources as can be seen in the "Works Cited and Consulted" page. Primary sources (interviews, first-hand reports, etc.) were used where no work is cited in the chapter on "Present Day Women of Revival".

Contributors:
Rev. 'Gatebreaker' G. Reid
Apostle Dr. E. E. Collins
Bishop O. Reid
Bishop N. Evans
Rev. S. McKoy
Bishop K. D. Collins

Paperback ISBN-13: 978-1-6628-4317-4
Ebook ISBN-13: 978-1-6628-4318-1

Table of Contents

ACKNOWLEDGMENT IX
INTRODUCTION. XI
SOUL-SAVING WOMEN IN THE GOSPELS 1
GIFTED WOMEN OF THE EARLY CHURCH. 5
A BIBLICAL DEFENSE OF WOMEN MINISTERS 9
NINETEENTH CENTURY FIRE WOMEN. 25
TWENTIETH CENTURY WOMEN OF REVIVAL 39
PRESENT DAY WOMEN OF REVIVAL 45
BEWARE OF JEZEBEL OBSTRUCTION. 67
WOMEN OF ZION, ARISE! 73
SPIRITUAL RIOT 81
CONCLUSION. 85

ACKNOWLEDGMENT

I THANK GOD for the Women of The Harvest!

If I perish! I perish! (Esther 4:16). These were the words of Esther who was made a queen for the purpose of saving her people from the hands of the enemy. A story of self-denial in a time when she had the opportunity to be like all the other women in the kingdom. She chose to be obedient to her uncle who encouraged her not to be silent but to speak to the king. The burden of her people was heavy upon her as she foresaw the future without her nation.

Should we keep quiet while worldly women entrap millions to go to hell by deceptive, sexual, provocative, lustful, and adulterous ways? The world does endorse such behaviors and elevate their voices through films, music, media, books, and shows. Yet those that stand and preach the infallible Word of God with Pentecostal fire are frowned upon and condemned by the world and unfortunately by some church leaders.

I thank God for the Women of Harvest Army Church International who have been preaching the gospel of Jesus Christ for the past 27 years. We greatly appreciate the founding vessel, Bishop Dr. K.D. Collins and co-founding vessel Apostle Dr. E.E. Collins who have been prime examples for us to follow, igniting the fire of God in our lives. We are the end time firebrands that prophesy and preach the word in every corner of the earth. Biblically trained and equipped to establish the end time purpose of our Lord and Savior, we spread the gospel of Jesus

Christ. Through persecution and resentment, we continue to thrive in the faith knowing that God is able, choosing not to eat the meat of the world, but endure the cross. We preach and prophesy to reach the lost at any cost.

Found throughout street corners across the world with the message of hope and deliverance, soul-saving women are challenging the culture and stepping into purpose as women of destiny. Her pulpit is in the streets of the world as she utters her voice for men, women, boys, and girls to "come to Jesus before it's too late". Preaching from the dangerous streets of New York while she cries *"repent for the kingdom of God is at hand"*; or the forgotten streets of Africa where she leaves the four walls of the church and run in the street to tell about the soon coming king. Women that refuse to stay at ease until their house is serving God. We are the Women of the Harvest that are born to bear and chosen to care. The fire of God is shut up in our bones and we refuse to relent until every soul is reached.

INTRODUCTION

WOMEN ARE THE WOMB for God's purpose! Throughout the Bible, God employs women as instruments of His plan. He raised up Miriam to be in leadership with Moses and Aaron (Micah 6:4). She sang songs of deliverance unto the Lord as she led the people of God into victory. The prophetess Deborah, who was also a judge in Israel, went before Barak in war. She then stated, *"I will surely go with thee: notwithstanding the journey that thou takest shall not be for thine honour; for the LORD shall sell Sisera into the hand of a woman"* (Judges 4:9 KJV). There are other heroic women like Rahab who hid the spies on top of the wall and in doing so saved her family (Joshua 6:17). And Jochebed saved her baby, Moses, by placing him in a basket to spare him from the wrath of Pharaoh, not knowing that Moses would bring a great deliverance unto Israel (Exodus; 2:1-4; Exodus 6:20). The Old Testament speaks of many other women that left their mark and played a part in saving the children of Israel.

Jesus was a master at equipping the forsaken and the rejected. He included women throughout his ministry. He elevated women, such as the woman found in adultery in John chapter 8, or the woman with the issue of blood (Mark 5:25-34). No other so-called religion on earth has equipped women like the gospel of Jesus Christ have done, not only to be productive human beings but also to spiritually reproduce and fill the earth with God's purpose.

The Bible is unparalleled among ancient books in elevating the status of women. No other book has given women more hope, security, boldness, recognition, and empowerment. Jesus publicly spoke and encouraged women although the Jewish traditions of the time forbade it. When a woman was taken in adultery, Jesus stood as her representative and defended her before the accusers. Jesus knew how to restore the identity of broken and fallen women.

Women were among them when Jesus commanded that they should not leave Jerusalem until they receive the promise from the father (Act 1:14). On the day of Pentecost, the promise fell from heaven, and they were all filled with the Holy Ghost. All, including the women, spoke in tongues, prophesied and proclaimed the good news. Therefore, in these last days before Christ makes his appearance, women must rise and preach the gospel and usher in the greatest revival known to humanity.

In today's world, we often see women engaging in all manner of positions. It is through Christianity that women started to recognize their identity in a world that did not accept them as equals. However, the most significant place of a woman rests in the call of God on her life. In this book, we will show the rise of women from the time of Christ until now that God has used to bring souls to Christ, including female Preachers, Pastors, Evangelists, Prophetesses, and Apostles. These women are Christ-followers that carry the burden to bring mankind back to fellowship with God. Although some still fail to acknowledge the full calling of God upon women, God has chosen women to be instruments of His revival.

As we look at women throughout history, we acknowledge and show how God has used these women to save souls and to impact the body of Christ significantly. Just as the characters of the Bible, some of these women may have faults, and or have made mistakes in their life or ministry. Therefore, do not view our acknowledgment of how God has used these women as an endorsement of all their actions. Instead, we present these ladies as evidence that God uses women in ministry to save souls and bring revival.

SOUL-SAVING WOMEN IN THE GOSPELS

THE WOMAN OF SAMARIA JOHN 4:1-42

"COME SEE A MAN" are the words that flowed from the lips of the woman of Samaria following her encounter with Jesus Christ. This woman's testimony is a story of hope, restoration, grace, compassion, and revival. These words echo throughout history, revealing the grace of God to women across the world.

How could Jesus speak to this woman? This is what her critics pondered when they found out that Jesus passed through Samaria and met this woman at Jacob's well. As Jesus spoke to the Samaritan woman, her desire to drink from the spiritual well rose as she longed for waters that could quench the thirst in her soul. Observing that she was open to the truth, Jesus started to tell her the truth about her life.

Yes, when God calls us He first unveils our lives so we can become believers in Christ. He proceeded to teach her about true worship. Jesus said to her "God is a Spirit and they that worship him must worship him in spirit and in truth" (verse 24). This was the commencement of a well springing forth inside of her. As he continued speaking Jesus made a ground shaking declaration to the woman in John 4:26 "I that speak to you am He." How revolutionary were those words in that time; the Son of God revealed his identity to an adulterous, non-Jewish woman. As Jesus showed himself to her, the disciples came back from town only to find him standing by a woman. They never engaged her in any conversation or asked Christ what he was doing speaking to the woman. But having caught the revelation, the woman dropped the water pot she was carrying and ran into the city.

As she ran to the city she carried a burden for the lost souls. She was burdened with the mission for souls. How could she not share it with Samaria and the world? How could she stay silent and complacent when many were worshipping idols and not knowing the true living God? She went on a soul-saving mission. Her mouth became a weapon against the religious traditions and false worship. As she approached the city she could not help but to cry aloud, sparing nothing. Souls were dying in this town and the men needed an awakening call from God, and the women needed to hear her testimony so they could live godly lives. She became a soul winning soldier as many flocked to Jesus because of her confession as written in John 4:29: "Come, see a man, which told me all things that ever I did: is not this the Christ?"

As she made this proclamation the men in the city came out and met with Christ (John 4:30). With Christ-given grace and mercy, this woman became a light to the world by breaking the barriers of her time and preaching the gospel of Jesus Christ. Jesus said to the disciples "Lift up your eyes, and look on the fields; for they are white already to harvest" (John 4:35) He continued and said, "I sent you to reap that whereon ye bestowed no labour: other men laboured, and ye are entered into their labours" (John 4:38). The disciples received a mighty harvest because of a woman that carried a burden for her city and preached the gospel. In the book of Acts chapter 9:30, the Bible reveals that a mighty revival came to Samaria as souls came to the Lord. Her interaction with Jesus at the well and subsequent testimony to the people of the city likely laid the foundation for the establishment of a church in Samaria as described in the book of Acts.

Today her story resounds in millions of sermons, thousands of songs and hundreds of languages. Her testimony is still alive, and so her running was not in vain. Many have been encouraged by her boldness not to keep quiet. Full of compassion for the lost and a soul winner, she was a symbol for all women that would choose the living water. She was the first woman in biblical record to take the gospel of Jesus to the streets. We are the women of God that are left to continue what she has started.

MARY MAGDALENE

Jesus was not afraid to allow women to stand out and make a difference. The ladies that followed him knew all too well that he was equipping them to change the world. These female followers can rightly be called Disciples of Christ since they followed him, and sacrificed their belongings to be with him (Luke 8:1-3; Mark 15:40-41; Matthew 27:55,56, 61).

As Jesus traveled in different communities he brought along his disciples and among them were Joanna, Susanna, and Mary Magdalene. Luke 8:2 tells us Jesus expelled seven demons from Mary Magdalene. Jesus implanted the call of God in Mary Magdalene's life through his ministry in her life. She followed him from town to cities as she watched him teach, heal the sick and gave hope to souls. The purpose of Christ and His desire for the lost was birthed within her. Christ came to save the world, and she was compelled to be a disciple and supporter of Christ's ministry (Luke 8:3). His teachings strengthened and empowered her to follow in a time when the twelve male disciples fled because of fear of the Jews. Mary Magdalene remained at the feet of the cross and ministered to Christ at his crucifixion. (John 19:25; Matthew 27:56).

As she wept regarding the body of her missing Savior, Jesus suddenly appeared and said: "woman" (John 20:15). The first Adam called Eve "woman" saying that she was taken from man, and the name that was given to her became tainted with sin. A curse was placed upon her name, and she has been covered with shame and resentment. Her given name was Mary, but Jesus called her by the name she was given from the beginning, signifying that He had restored her. Jesus is the second Adam who came to restore what was stolen. Therefore, Jesus said to her "woman," now restored by the power of the resurrection.

She was the first eyewitness to the resurrection that would set the captives free. In a time when Jewish customs held that women should be silent in public, Jesus sent her on a mission to the male disciples to declare to them His resurrection. A woman was chosen to run with the most powerful message given to humanity. God sent a woman with a message of restoration and revival. What a bruising to the devil that first had deceived the woman!

She refused to let the religious, political and cultural laws keep her silent as she ran with the message of the Risen Christ. The resurrection message opened up a new chapter for the followers of Christ, a commission to declare the resurrection. Thousands of years later the voice of Mary Magdalene echoes across the world "He is risen".

GIFTED WOMEN OF THE EARLY CHURCH

FOUNDATIONAL LEADERS AND PASTORS

THE EARLY CHURCH began with foundational women of God. Act 1:14 states, "These all continued with one accord in prayer and supplication, with the women, and Mary the mother of Jesus, and with his brethren." Along with the twelve disciples, there were also female Disciples of Christ who were present following Jesus' ascension and received the baptism of the Holy Spirit with utterance in other tongues (Acts 2). Having witnessed Christ resurrection, and empowered by the Holy Spirit, they were spreading the gospel of Christ. Even at Pentecost, they spoke in other tongues the wonders of God. Other women that came to faith in Christ in the early church would also become early church leaders and preachers of the gospel of Jesus Christ.

Evidently, women were active in ministry and leadership in the missions and epistles of Paul. Arriving in Philippi in one of his mission trips, Paul's first connection was with a group of women at a place of prayer. As they prayed, Paul engaged the women in conversation. As he spoke, a lady named Lydia carefully listened. The scripture said she was a "worshiper of God"(Act 16:14). God opened her heart to the gospel. Lydia was the first convert of Paul in Philippi.

God, knowing her desire, opened her heart that she would receive Paul's teachings. The same spirit that was on Paul came upon this woman once she surrendered her heart to Jesus. She and her household were baptized after receiving the teachings of the Apostle Paul. After baptism, she convinced Paul's company to stay at her house (Act 16:15). Her influential character is evident since the scriptures tell us that she persuaded them to stay in her home, saying, *"If ye have judged me to be faithful to the Lord, come into my house, and abide there"* (Acts 16:15). It was through Paul's teachings that she strengthened the other new converts.

Afterward, Paul and Silas were thrown into prison for their ministry. Upon being freed from prison, they entered the house of Lydia and comforted the brethren and then left (Acts 16:40). Paul trusted her to nourish and mentor the believers. Paul did not doubt as he encouraged them and departed with peace of mind. Paul had imparted the gospel into her life, birthing ministerial gifts within her. As a foundational leader of the church in her house, she was a teacher, a mentor as she led many to the Lord. Her submission to the Word of God brought her household to their knees as they surrendered their life to Jesus Christ. Paul trusted her with the gospel, and she became the leader of the church in her house and played a significant role in the foundational structure of the Philippian church.

WOMEN AMONG THE APOSTLESHIP
Roman 16:7 Salute Andronicus and Junia, my kinsmen, and my fellow-prisoners, who are of note among the apostles, who also were in Christ before me.

Junia was a noteworthy apostle. An apostle is a sent one. So, it is safe to conclude that similarly to the male apostles, the hand of God was on Junia to preach the gospel in new territories, plant and establish churches, teach and preach, perform miracles, and win souls to Christ.

Paul gave salutation to her, which is a sign of honor and respect. Paul highly regarded her. He honored her work by calling it "of note among the Apostles" which meant that her ministry and the work that she performed was outstanding and exemplary.

She was also a fellow prisoner with Paul. Paul was beaten, shipwrecked, placed in prison and endured hardship for the gospel of Jesus Christ. However, he still acknowledged a woman as a fellow prisoner.

The apostles knew about her outstanding work within the ministry, and God allowed her name to be placed in scripture to break the barriers that have been placed upon women, releasing them to fulfill their purpose in ministry. Paul mentioning Junia is a confirmation that women that are called to such office should arise and fulfill the will of God.

God has women whom he has sent, and commissioned as apostles, but have resisted the call because of ministry walls placed upon women. But, millions are going to hell on a daily basis so how can we, the mothers in Zion, watch and say, 'but we are not sent?" Just like Junia, we must take the mantle and carry it with grace and humility.

WOMEN AS MINISTERS

Phebe was a (servant) deacon in the church of Cenchrea (Romans 16:1-2). Paul's announcement of Phebe was warm and brotherly because he referred to her as "our sister", but he quickly announced her position as a servant or a minister in the church. She was of value to the work in the church. He affirms that she should be received in the Lord as a saint. This woman was to be received with honor and respect. She was trusted and valued. He instructed the Roman church that she should be assisted in whatever was needed. Paul was ensuring that the church would show her honor in caring for her. In Romans 16:2, Paul said she is a succorer of many and also himself. A succorer is a person who helps others in need. Phebe made herself available to those in need including Paul; She ministered to the needs of the apostles and brethren in Christ.

She was a vanguard who was entrusted with the responsibility of delivering the epistle to the church in Rome. Possibly, she even publicly read Paul's epistle to the Roman church. She was a soul winner and did everything within her power to make sure that those that became converts were being taught and growing in their new found faith.

PRISCILLA THE PASTOR, TEACHER AND ITINERANT MINISTER

Apostle Paul came in contact with Priscilla and her husband, Aquila at Corinth. He met the husband and wife at a time when Paul was undergoing persecution. Paul stated in the book of Romans that they were his helpers in Jesus Christ (Romans 16:3). She and her husband were leading the church in their home in Ephesus. Both Priscilla and her husband would give their life for Paul and he was grateful for them, but it was Priscilla's name that was usually first mentioned in his writings (Act 18:18-19, 26: Roman.16:3; 2 Tim.4:19). This reveals that she played a prominent role in the ministry. When the great Apollos came to town (Act 18:24-26), a great scholar, fervent in spirit, and mighty in scripture, he expounded on the word but according to the baptism of John. It was Priscilla and her husband that came to the aid of Apollos and explained unto him the way of God more perfectly. This means she and her husband were teaching Apollos the baptism of water and the Holy Ghost through Jesus Christ. Her powerful teachings on Christ allowed the disciples, in a city called Achaia, to be more receptive toward him. Apollos now had the power to convince the Jews through the scriptures that Jesus Christ was the Messiah.

Priscilla was a teacher, pastor, and a foundational leader in the early church. She moved with grace and compassion for the lost. She was teaching and ministering in a time when idol worship was prevalent in the city of Ephesus (Act 19:35), yet this woman of God upheld the teaching of the Lord Jesus and led many to understand the purpose of the cross of Christ.

A BIBLICAL DEFENSE OF WOMEN MINISTERS

CAN WOMEN BE PASTORS AND LEAD IN THE CHURCH?

TODAY THERE ARE STILL CHURCHES that prohibit women from preaching in their pulpits. Some churches have acknowledged the spiritual gifts given to many women in the body of Christ and allow them to minister in various capacities but still prohibit them from pastoring or having positions of leadership in the local church. Two scriptures are often used to prevent women in ministry: I Corinthians 14:34 - 35 and I Timothy 2:11-12.

However, to answer a critical question like this, it is imperative that we look at the general view of scripture, not just a few isolated verses. Is the general view of scripture against women in leading positions in the church, or do we see a general tendency in female leadership? Here you will see three things:

(1) There is evidence of female spiritual leadership throughout the Bible, (2) That the general overview of scripture strongly supports women in ministry leadership, (3) The Bible reveals a pattern of God using the "unqualified", and "prohibited".

EVIDENCE FROM THE OLD TESTAMENT

There are examples of female leaders throughout the Bible. The Old Testament gives examples of women who provided spiritual and governmental leadership to the people of Israel. First, there is Miriam, who was a prophetess (Exodus 15:20). She is also named as one of the top three leaders in Israel in *Micah 6:4 For I brought thee up out of the land of Egypt, and redeemed thee out of the house of servants; and I sent before thee Moses, Aaron, and Miriam.* Named among Moses and Aaron, the scripture states that Miriam was "sent before" Israel. Miriam was counted as one of the spiritual leaders of the called out people of Israel.

Deborah was also a spiritual leader in Israel and governed the people. She served Israel in the office of a prophet. She was also one of the judges of Israel. The people of Israel came to her for judgment concerning their civil issues according to Judges 4:4. Her able leadership prompted the army captain, Barak, to request for her to go with him to war, saying *"If thou wilt go with me, then I will go: but if thou wilt not go with me, then I will not go"* (Judges 4:6).

Huldah was a prophetess in Judah in the time of King Josiah. She was a notable prophetess since Hilkiah the priest, and the appointed officials of the king went to her on behalf of king Josiah to inquire of the Lord (2 Kings 22:12-20). She responded and gave them a word from the Lord, which the king responded to and followed. Her spiritual leadership, as a spokeswoman for God, was fully recognized and acknowledged. The prophet Jeremiah was a contemporary with Huldah. Yet Huldah was consulted, and not Jeremiah; this reveals that she had a notable reputation as a prophetess. .

So far, we see that Miriam, Deborah, and Huldah were prophetesses and spiritual leaders in Israel. A couple of things to recognize from the above female leaders from the Old Testament:

1) **They operated in the office of a prophet.** Therefore, they did not just give prophetic utterance but were recognized prophets

that the Israelites would come to for a word from God, and or for spiritual guidance. Their prophecies were recognized as coming from God. They were known as spiritual leaders because they consistently gave prophetic utterances and revelations to guide the people and the nation.

2) **They provided spiritual guidance and leadership.** Miriam led the children of Israel in praise and worship in Exodus 15:20. Deborah provided judicial and governmental guidance as seen in Judges 4:4.

3) **Their ministry and leadership were widely known and respected.** Their ministry was not private or behind closed doors; their ministry was nationally recognized and acknowledged. They were performing public ministry to the masses.

4) There are other female prophets mentioned that shows a general acceptance of prophetic female leaders. Noadiah, the prophetess, is mentioned among other prophets in Nehemiah 6:14, although she seemed to have been a false prophet, it still shows a general acceptance of female prophetic leaders. Also, Isaiah's wife appears to have been a prophetess (Isaiah 8:3).

It is unlikely that God allowed women to hold positions of spiritual leadership under the old covenant, but then reduced their ministry activity in the New Testament. Biblically there seems to be an increase in the amount and type of people God uses in ministry as we progress in prophetic history. Consider for instance that Moses envisioned the prophetic anointing being poured out on a broader scale among the people of God, saying *"would God that **all** the LORD's people were prophets, and that the LORD would put his spirit upon them!"* (Numbers 11:29 emphasis added). And Joel did prophesy that the Spirit would be poured out upon *all flesh...and daughters would prophesy, and....handmaids would prophesy* (Joel 2: 28 - 29).

EVIDENCE FROM THE NEW TESTAMENT

In fact, the New Testament records women prophesying, and being prophetesses.

- Mary prophesied (Luke 1:46-55).
- Elisabeth prophesied (Luke 1:41-42).
- Anna had a prophetic revelation (Luke 2:36-38).
- Philip's four daughters were prophetesses (Acts 21:9).

Prophecy is one of the spiritual gifts. God does not discriminate between male and female in the distribution of the gifts of the Spirit. In like manner, the ministry gifts given to the church has no reference of being only for male, but Christ gave gifts some apostles, prophets, evangelists, pastors, and teachers for the benefit of the body of Christ (Ephesians 4:11-12).

In the New Testament, there is mention of female apostles, prophets, evangelists, pastors, teachers, and other ministry leaders some of which have already been mentioned in this book. These will be explored further.

JUNIA: THE APOSTLE

Junia in Romans 16:7 is mentioned as notable among the apostles. Interestingly, the fourth-century bishop of Constantinople, John Chrysostom in his homilies on Romans, commented on Romans 16:7 saying, "oh how great is the devotion of this woman, that she should be even counted worthy of the appellation of apostle!" (Schaff).

In fact, the consensus in church tradition up until the Middle Ages was that Junia was a female apostle (Scot). Origen of Alexandria, a church father from the second century considered Junia to be a female apostle, and Jerome of the fourth also considered Junia to be female.

DAUGHTERS OF PHILIP: THE PROPHETS
Acts 21:9 And the same man had four daughters, virgins, which did prophesy.

The daughters of Philip were prophetesses. Prophesying was common in the early church as seen in I Corinthians 11 and I Corinthians 14 among other scriptures in the book of Acts. The fact that Philip's daughters are explicitly mentioned implies that they most likely operated in the office of a prophet. The scripture indicates that they prophesy as if this was an area they regularly operated in and were known for as such they seemed to have been recognized as prophetesses. This follows in the line of other women in the office of a prophet in the Bible such as Miriam, Deborah, Huldah, and Anna.

Eusebius the fourth-century church historian also holds that the daughters of Philip were prophets even naming them among early church prophets such as Agabus, Judas, and Silas (Eusebius of Caesarea; Acts 11:27-28; Acts 15:22, 27);

ANNA: THE PROPHETESS

Anna was a prophetess who spent all her time in the temple. She was known as a prophet according to the scripture. Therefore, her prophecies would take place regularly within the temple. When the baby Jesus was brought into the temple, the scripture says that *"she coming in that instant gave thanks likewise unto the Lord, and spake of him to all them that looked for redemption in Jerusalem."* (Luke 2:38). She had been prophesying concerning Christ to as many as came in the temple. Some say that women should not speak in a church, yet this woman, Anna, was used by God to utter in the temple regularly.

LYDIA: THE PASTOR

Lydia was a convert in Paul's ministry at Philippi. She seemed to have been the leader of the home church given that the brethren met in her home. *Acts 16:40 And they went out of the prison, and entered into the house of Lydia: and when they had seen the brethren, they comforted them, and departed.* It was the norm for churches to meet in homes. Lydia led the church in her home, and so functioned as a pastor.

PHEBE: THE MINISTER

I commend unto you Phebe our sister, which is a servant of the church which is at Cenchrea: That ye receive her in the Lord, as becometh saints, and that ye assist her in whatsoever business she hath need of you: for she hath been a succourer of many, and of myself also. (Romans 16:1).

Phebe is called a servant of the church, which has also been translated a deacon or even minister. She helped many including Paul. Phebe was a leader in the church who had ministered to many.

PRISCILLA: THE PASTOR-TEACHER

Acts 18:26 And he began to speak boldly in the synagogue: whom when Aquila and Priscilla had heard, they took him unto them, and expounded unto him the way of God more perfectly.

The above scripture speaks of Priscilla as having expounded on the scriptures to Apollos along with her husband Aquila. They were doing ministry together. There is nothing in the scripture to conclude that Priscilla was not teaching along with her husband. In fact, in the Greek, as reflected in other translations other than the KJV, Priscilla's name is mentioned before her husband. It seems that Priscilla was a teacher and accepted lecturer of the word, functioned in the pastoral role, and also ministered in other churches.

I Corinthians 16:9 The churches of Asia salute you. Aquila and Priscilla salute you much in the Lord, with the church that is in their house.

Again here, the lady Priscilla is mentioned along with her husband as leaders of the church in their house. They both sent their greetings and revealed that Priscilla ministered to the church in her home along with her husband.

CO-WORKERS
Romans 16:3-5 Greet Priscilla and Aquila my helpers in Christ Jesus: 4 "Who have for my life laid down their own necks: unto whom not only I give thanks, but also all the churches of the Gentiles. Likewise greet the church that is in their house."

Here in the book of Romans, the Apostle Paul sends greetings to Priscilla and Aquila calling them his helpers in Christ. The Greek word translated helpers is συνεργούς, transliterated 'synergous', which means **"fellow workers"**. Paul considered Aquilla a fellow worker or a **co-worker** in the Lord. He placed both Priscilla and her husband on equal footing in the ministry along with him. Paul also called Timothy and Titus fellow-workers (Romans 16:21).

Priscilla was a woman that laid down her life to minister the gospel and in strengthening the churches since Paul states that all the churches of the Gentiles are thankful for them. Therefore, Priscilla led a house church functioning as a pastor, preached the gospel, and ministered among the Gentile churches. Consequently, she functioned in the teaching ministry, pastoral ministry, and the ministry of the evangelist.

There are other New Testament examples of women in ministry. These few are mentioned to show women operating in the pastoral gift and other leading gifts. The Holy Spirit distributes the gifts among the body of Christ as He wills.

GENERAL SCRIPTURAL INSTRUCTION:
With the pouring out of the Spirit of God at Pentecost, spiritual gifts would be manifested among all the people of God both male and female as alluded to in Joel prophecy in *Joel 2:28: And it shall come to pass afterward, that I will pour out my spirit upon all flesh; and your*

sons and your daughters shall prophesy, your old men shall dream dreams, your young men shall see visions. Here we see that the manifestation of spiritual gifts would not be barred by age, sex, or social status. We can say that the manifestation of spiritual gifts is Ageless, Genderless, and Classless. The scripture stresses that it would be both sons and daughters, and male and female servants.

In 1 Corinthians 12:7, the scripture states, *Now to each one the manifestation of the Spirit is given for the common good.* The manifestation of the Spirit is given to each one of us. There are no gender restrictions given as to who would receive the manifestation of the Spirit. The manifestation is given to each one for the benefit of the body of Christ. Among the manifestations listed are speaking gifts, revelatory gifts, and working gifts. The speaking gifts being prophecy, tongues, and interpretation of tongues. The revelatory gifts being word of wisdom, word of knowledge, and discerning of spirits. The working gifts being faith, working of miracles, and gifts of healings. The Spirit distributes the gifts to each person according to the will of God (I Corinthians 12:11). Since there are no restrictions given to women in receiving the speaking gifts, we must conclude that women would operate in the gifts of prophecy, tongues, and interpretation of tongues within the church. This falls in agreement with Joel 2:28-29. Therefore, by the Spirit's prompting, it is necessary that women publicly speak in the church to edify all.

Furthermore, 1 Corinthians 12:28-31 states, *And God hath set some in the church, first apostles, secondarily prophets, thirdly teachers, after that miracles, then gifts of healings, helps, governments, diversities of tongues. Are all apostles? Are all prophets? Are all teachers? Are all workers of miracles? Have all the gifts of healing? Do all speak with tongues? Do all interpret? But covet earnestly the best gifts: and yet shew I unto you a more excellent way.*

Here Paul gives a different list of gifts including apostles, prophets, teachers, helps, and governments. Paul even told the believers to desire the best gifts; again, with no gender restrictions given. Some of these gifts are similar to the ministry gifts listed in Ephesians 4:11 *And he gave some, apostles; and some, prophets; and some, evangelists; and some, pastors and teachers;* That scripture passage also states, *But unto every one of us is given grace according to the measure of the gift of Christ* (Ephesians 4:7). Revealing here that the ministry gifts are given according to the will of God to any believer, with no gender restrictions. The scripture did not state everyone except women, but instead *everyone*, *each* of us, and *all*. Apostleship, pasturing, teaching, and evangelizing are among the spiritual gifts given to the body and can, therefore, operate among women. Again, spiritual gifts are released through the outpouring of the Spirit of God so the prophecy of Joel reveals that there would be an explosion of spiritual gifts among God's people among both men and women.

Building on this there are many scriptures revealing the necessity of all believers using their gifts in the church and ministering to each other.

The Bible teaches the following concerning all believers, male and female:

- Desire spiritual gifts (I Corinthians 14:1). Remember that the gifts listed by Paul in 1Corinthians 12 include gifts that would involve leading and or public speaking in a church setting such as an apostle, prophet, and teacher.

- Excel in gifts that edify the church (1Corinthians 14:12). This would mean that women that desire to follow this scripture would be ministering and speaking in the church.

- The scripture speaks of **all** prophesying in the church (1Corinthians 14:24). Again, this would include women prophesying in the church.

- Everyone should come to church services ready to utilize their spiritual gift, and minister to each other (1Corinthians 14:26).

- We must minister according to the gifts given to us. This includes prophecy, teaching, leading, among others. There are no gender restrictions given (Roman 12:5-8).

- We should all faithfully use whatever gifts God has given us. Again, no gender restrictions are provided.

All of the above scriptures are written to the general Body of Christ, including both men and women. God instructs both males and females on the spiritual gifts, to desire them, and utilize them. The list of gifts includes areas where church leadership and or public speaking in a church would be necessary. In light of Joel 2:28, that stresses the pouring out of the Spirit on all flesh, this is an expected progression in the distribution of spiritual gifts of all types to both men and women. Female believers reading these texts have strong reasons to believe these scriptures apply to them because the Spirit has been poured out on them as with male believers: they are one with men in Christ according to Galatians 3:28; there are examples of women in ministry throughout the Old and New Testament, and the scriptures speak of everyone and all. All means all.

The examples above also show that female ministry and leadership was a norm in the early church evidenced by the ministry of women mentioned explicitly in the book of Acts, and the Apostle Paul naming and greeting women in ministry. Furthermore, with the prophecy of Joel 2:28 showing an explosion of Spirit gifting among both men and women, we should expect women ministry and spiritual leadership to increase beyond the scope of the Old Testament. The Old Testament already named a few women with spiritual gifting and leadership, and we should expect that to accelerate in the new covenant.

In light of the weight of scriptures showing God setting up female leadership among the Israelites of the Old Testament, and the church of the New Testament receiving them, we should allow to bear weight on the answer to the question of can women pastor or lead in the church.

Furthermore, we must also consider the general progression in scripture of widespread increase in ministry among all people. With that in mind let us look at I Corinthians 14:34-35 and I Timothy 2:11-12. The intention here is not an exhaustive exegesis of the text but rather to show the inefficiency of the current application of these two scriptures, and the necessity of appealing to the general view of scripture concerning women in leadership.

1 Corinthians 14:34-35 Let your women keep silence in the churches: for it is not permitted unto them to speak; but they are commanded to be under obedience, as also saith the law. And if they will learn anything, let them ask their husbands at home: for it is a shame for women to speak in the church.

The most natural and literal interpretation of the above scripture is that women should not speak within the church. Anything they need to ask can be done at home. Other interpretations or conclusions by those who believe that women cannot have leadership roles in ministry are insufficient when considering the literal words of the passage:

- Women cannot pastor a church
- Women cannot teach
- Women can only teach other women

All of the above interpretations fail to realize that the scripture states they should be silent and not allowed to speak. Literally, it would mean women cannot speak at all in a church setting; It even states it is a shame for women to do so. However, most churches that forbid women from holding leading positions in the church do allow women to speak in the church in some capacity, such as Sunday School teachers, women ministries, and such the like. This allowance would still not be following a literal interpretation of 1 Corinthians 14:34 - 35. A literal interpretation would mean they cannot speak in the church.

Should we then take this scripture and allow it to carry the weight in our answer to the question, should women lead in the church? Rightly dividing the scriptures, it seems God intended for women to speak in the church for ministry. The same Apostle Paul, who wrote the letter to the Corinthians, in the same epistle gave instructions for women to pray and prophesy within the church setting. *I Corinthians 11:5 But every woman that prayeth or prophesieth with her head uncovered dishonoureth her head: for that is even all one as if she were shaven.* This scripture reveals that Paul expected women to pray and prophesy in the church, and had clear instructions for the manner in which they should do it. And, from the context, we know that he was dealing with them prophesying and praying in the church since it is the same chapter and section of the epistle where he deals with orderly worship and ministry within the church.

The same chapter containing the prohibition on woman to speak, 1 Corinthians 14, in previous verses encourage all the saints to minister one to another and prophesy. There seems to be some contradiction in Paul's words, on the one hand, saying it is a shame for women to speak in the church, while at other times instructing women on how to rightly prophesy in the church. Since God's word is not contradictory, the problem must lie in our understanding of the passage; either we are missing some aspect of the meaning of the scripture due to differences in the culture at the time, or Paul's statement here is limited to a specific situation or time. Therefore, it is misguided to allow this single verse to guide our answer to the question of women ministry in the church.

I Timothy 2:11-12 Let the woman learn in silence with all subjection. But I suffer not a woman to teach, nor to usurp authority over the man, but to be in silence.

This scripture also seems to echo 1 Corinthians 14:34-35. It appears to forbid women from teaching and having any positions of leadership over men. There are a few things that should be considered about this passage: It is a radical position for the time for women to be allowed to learn. For women to learn in silence and submission does not prohibit them from doing ministry in a church.

The prohibition to teach seems connected to usurping authority. It is wrong for women to usurp authority to teach. Usurp is to take dominion or to overthrow the authority of another to gain authority. It would be wrong for a woman to usurp a man's authority as the head of the household or a man's authority as given by God in any setting.

When a woman leads by the Spirit, she is not taking dominion or overthrowing an authority not given to her. Instead, she is leading through the gift God has bestowed. In the case of the Spirit's empowerment and enablement, there is no instruction for women to be silent. In the context of the home, a woman that is a pastor cannot usurp her husband's authority as head of the house. In a church context, a gifted female pastor, evangelist, prophetess, or apostle should not usurp the authority of men that God has placed over her; however, she should faithfully utilize the gift that God has imparted in her life. Also, a woman that seeks to overthrow the authority of her leader is operating in a Jezebel spirit not the Spirit of God. (More will be said about the Jezebel spirit later in this book).

Therefore, usurping authority means that women should not rebelliously take charge or take dominion over a male leader, which is different from God equipping a woman for spiritual leadership. God gives leadership gifts and the church acknowledges the gifts; usurping authority is taking what is not yours. I Timothy 2:11-12 is limited to a rebellious taking of authority, and or usurping a man's authority in the home or the order of creation.

Here again, we must consider the totality of scripture including examples of women in positions of spiritual leadership throughout the Old and New Testament and the general teachings of the Bible that spiritual gifts should be operating among all believers - male and female.

We need to look through the lens of all of scripture, and not just make conclusions from these two sole scripture passages in I Corinthians 14:34-35, and I Timothy 2:11-12. Paul's writing here should be weighed upon in the light of the general view of scripture in support of female public ministry and spiritual leadership. We have examples to bear on this from the Old Testament to the New Testament as referenced above.

Besides, two biblical principles should supersede any seeming ministry restriction from 1Corinthians 14:34-35 or I Timothy 2:11-12: need and time. Therefore, 1 Corinthians 14:34-35 and I Timothy 2:11-12 would need to be seen as limited to that time (the specific time of Paul's writing), and or limited in scope (to that particular church, or situation he was dealing with). The need for more people in ministry and the time that we are living in calls for many more women to arise in ministry activity and leadership.

1) **Need**: Throughout scripture God has used those considered unqualified to fill a need in the fulfillment of his purpose. He used a donkey to speak to the prophet Balaam when Balaam could not perceive God's will (Numbers 22:21-39). Jesus told the Pharisees that if the people stopped shouting Hosanna, the rocks would cry out (Luke 19:40). Mary Magdalene was the first woman to spread the message of Christ's resurrection; the men were not available (Mark 16:9-10). To fill a need, it seems God would use anyone; He would surely use a woman. If there is a need to be filled, God will raise up a woman to pastor, evangelize, teach, prophecy, and do apostolic work.

In Judges 4:9, the unwillingness of Barak to lead the Israeli army without the accompaniment of a woman, led to God using a woman to be the decisive factor in the victory of the war. The trepidation of the man opened the door for God to use a woman. Not to suggest that women can only operate in ministry leadership when men are unavailable, but that the need expedites the call for women to rise in the ministry.

Even when Jesus upheld that salvation was for the Jews, the steadfast faith of the Phoenician woman won the favor of Christ, and she received her request (Matthew 15:21-28). The persistence of the woman gave her access to divine favor, to which at first she was denied. Jesus spoke of how David ate of unleavened bread, which was unlawful, but due to the need, it was allowed. Gentiles were brought into the kingdom of God as the Jews rejected salvation. The unwillingness of the Jews opened the door to the Gentiles.

Following those examples and patterns, it seems God would use anyone, including women, to fill the need of advancing the kingdom of God. In the occasion of the unwillingness, or unavailability of men, in the event of lack of men, wouldn't God who had done similar things throughout history use a woman to fulfill his purpose?

2) **Time:** The progression of scripture reveals that as time gets closer to the coming of the Lord, there would be an increase in both men and women doing ministry. The widespread outpouring of the Spirit of God upon all flesh is the catalyst for a massive rise in ministry among both men and women. Joel 2:28-29 And it shall come to pass afterward, *that* I will pour out my spirit upon all flesh; and your sons and your daughters shall prophesy, your old men shall dream dreams, your young men shall see visions: And also, upon the servants and upon the handmaids in those days will I pour out my spirit.

The Spirit of God gives great emphasis to women prophesying. The scripture mentions not only sons but, specifically daughters. Secondly, not only servants but, specifically handmaids. The two verses show that God is intentionally stressing the presence of women in this prophetic revival. Isaiah calls forth for the women to arise until there is a mighty revival. *Isaiah 32:9,10,15 Rise up, ye women that are at ease; hear my voice, ye careless daughters; give ear unto my speech. 10: Many days and years shall ye be troubled, ye careless women: for the vintage shall fail, the gathering shall not come. 15: Until the spirit be poured upon us from on high, and the wilderness be a fruitful field, and the fruitful field be counted for a forest.* To usher in revival, women seem to have a prominent role. Huldah, the prophetess, was instrumental in igniting a revival in Judah instructing King Josiah to follow the teaching of the biblical scrolls he had found.

Romans 9:28 For he will finish the work, and cut it short in righteousness: because a short work will the Lord make upon the earth.

    To expedite the work of God, surely God will use women in the last days to accomplish his purpose.

    Woe to the men who hinder or frustrate the work of the Spirit of God upon and through women. Throughout the rest of the book, there are examples of women that are used by God to win souls and usher in revival. When they read the Bible, and heard God's call, they were moved to speak, not to be silent.

NINETEENTH CENTURY FIRE WOMEN

PHOEBE PALMER

IN A TIME when women in ministry were rare or confined to home and neighborhood meetings, Phoebe Palmer won thousands of souls to Christ in the United States, Canada, England, and other parts of Europe. She was an evangelist as she traveled and ministered at various camp meetings and similar settings. Both men and women, including denominational leaders, received her message. She was also a prolific writer and articulated her message of the second blessing through her writing. She championed the belief that the church should allow women to utilize their gifts in the church in her book, *The Promise of the Father*. The following is a quote from her book expressing the need for women to be in ministry:

"The church a potter's field where the gifts of women are buried! And how serious will be the responsibilities of that church which does not hasten to roll away the stone, and bring out these long-buried gifts...God has eminently endowed women with gilts for the social circle. He has given her the power of persuasion and the ability to captivate. Who may win souls to Christ, if she may not." (Palmer, Chapter 16, The Seal Broken)

Phoebe Palmer became the primary representative of the Holiness Movement in the nineteenth century at a time when not many women were recognized as leaders in ministry. She grew up in a strict Methodist home, born in New York to parents that were members of the Methodist Episcopal church ("Phoebe Worrall Palmer"). From the age of eleven, Phoebe was already demonstrating a radical commitment to Christ, even writing biblical poems (Howie).

Born Phoebe Worrall, she married Walter Palmer in 1827. They lost three of their first four children through different tragic means. Nevertheless, the grief of her loss moved Phoebe to a greater commitment to Christ. When the third child died, she proclaimed herself fully devoted to God and dead to sin.

Around 1835, she began to lead a meeting in her home called "Tuesday Meetings," that was first led by her sister Sarah. After Sarah moved out of the Palmer's house, Phoebe took leadership of the meetings. Initially, only women attended the meeting, but by 1839 it became open to both sexes. Due to its popularity, the meetings grew from a small group to thousands. These meetings became an essential part of the Holiness Movement. Soon, attendees from other denominations would come to the meeting, including Bishops, Pastors, and other Christian leaders.

Her ministry continued to expand along with her husband, and she soon became an itinerant preacher ministering at camp meetings and holiness revivals around the United States. Doors even began to open for her to minister in Canada, and later in England. Through her ministry, thousands of souls were won to Christ. Her vast ministry in her home, and preaching throughout the country and other parts of the world led to her being recognized as one of the main leaders of the Holiness Movement.

Her role as a leader of the Holiness Movement is evident in that she served as the leader of the National Camp Meeting Association for the Promotion of Holiness. Along with her husband in 1867 she established the National Association for the Promotion of Holiness, which became the catalyst for much of her revivalist travels and meetings. At first, she was a regular contributor to the Guide to Holiness, the leading publication of the Holiness Movement, but in 1862 she became the editor of the publication after her husband purchased it ("Phoebe Worrall Palmer").

She wrote many books including "The Way of Holiness", "Entire Devotion to God," and "Faith and its Effect." Her primary message was that sanctification, or the second blessing, was received through a declaration of faith in what the Word of God teaches.

AMANDA BERRY SMITH
"Lord I am willing to go just tell me where to go." – Amanda Berry Smith

Both her skin color and gender were barriers to entry into public Christian ministry, yet Amanda Berry Smith stood her ground and became a powerful force within her time. She was born as a slave in 1837, but during her childhood year's slavery was abolished (Smith). One day Amanda became sick, and while lying on her sick bed, God visited her in a dream. She saw herself preaching to lost souls at a tent meeting. After that experience, Amanda became a convert and an active advocate in the Holiness Movement when Phoebe Palmer was the leader of the meetings. She was the first African American woman to become a part of the National Holiness Movement. She became well known as she preached the gospel and sang songs on the street corners.

The Lord miraculously opened doors for public ministry through the African Methodist Church. Smith raised up the standard in the society and America as she brought both blacks and whites together in a time of segregation and poverty. Hundreds were converted in these meetings, and African Americans and whites alike honored her. The Lord expanded her ministry, and she was moved to take the gospel across the sea. In 1878, she traveled to England followed by India, Ireland, Scotland, and Africa, as an Independent Missionary (Smith). Although she was never officially ordained, through her obedience to the call of God she paved a pathway for women to rise in Christian leadership positions.

She was an evangelist, missionary and a preacher approved by God. Her book, "An Autobiography, The Story of the Lord's Dealings with Mrs. Amanda Smith" is an autobiography of Smith's life as a woman who despite the challenges rose beyond her race and preached the gospel in different continents. Although not well known she was one of the most radical evangelists of the 19th century.

In the introduction to her autobiography, the following is what Bishop Thoburn of India said about Mrs. Smith:

"During the seventeen years that I have lived in Calcutta, I have known many famous strangers to visit the city, some of whom attracted large audiences, but I have never known anyone who could draw and hold so large an audience as Mrs. Smith.

She assisted me both in the church and in open-air meetings, and never failed to display the peculiar tact for which she is remarkable.

I shall never forget one meeting, which we were holding in an open square, in the very heart of the city. It was at a time of no little excitement, and some Christian preachers had been roughly handled in the same square a few evenings before. I had just spoken myself, when I noticed a great crowd of men and boys, who had succeeded in breaking up a missionary's audience on the other side of the square, rushing towards us with loud cries and threatening gestures.

If left to myself I should have tried to gain the box on which the speakers stood, in order to command the crowd, but at the critical moment, our good Sister Smith knelt on the grass and began to pray. As the crowd rushed up to the spot, and saw her with her beaming face upturned to the evening sky, pouring out her soul in prayer, they became perfectly still, and stood as if transfixed to the spot! Not even a whisper disturbed the solemn silence, and when she had finished we had as orderly a meeting as if we had been within the four walls of a church! (Smith vii)."

Amanda Berry Smith, a woman of color, proved that the gospel of Jesus Christ is race-less, genderless, borderless as she stepped out on a mission to save souls. She spent an estimated two years in England, eighteen months in India and eight years in Africa. As a result of her mission work, thousands were touched and gave their hearts to the Lord. After her return to America, Dr. Theodore Ledyard Cuyler who was leading the largest Presbyterian Church invited her to preach. At the time his congregation held more than 4,000 members (Smith).

She lived the rest of her life preaching the gospel of Jesus Christ. She left her mark on a culture that denied her the very right to exist. But the Holy Spirit gave her access to every right to live by calling her to deliver souls by preaching the gospel.

MARIA WOODWORTH ETTER

"I started out after God baptized me in the Holy Ghost. I knew God was calling me for public service. I knew I would die unless God came to me like He did to the fishermen. I told the Lord if He would baptize me with power and knowledge that I would undertake the work. I would go to the ends of the earth and live a thousand years if I might take one soul to heaven. So the Lord wonderfully baptized me and sent me out." (Woodworth-Etter 50)

In her lifetime, she preached to crowds of over 25,000 people with many seeking to be healed by the power of God (Warner). The anointing would fall as she spoke the word of God and hundreds would fall to the floor asking God for forgiveness. Because of the anointing placed in her life, she was often scrutinized and received many threats against her life. Doctors along with other skeptics would line up in her meetings to come against her, and they were met with the power of God leaving confounded by what they saw.

Born on July 22, 1844, Maria Woodworth-Etter was no stranger to sorrow and heartache. Early in life, she experienced the death of her father. As a result, she had to work along with her siblings to support the family. Although she did not grow up in a Christian home, the family started attending a neighborhood church. When Maria heard the gospel, she was moved by the message. While being baptized, she had a conversion experience as the crowd reported that they saw lights all around her.

Although Maria felt the call of God to preach, she struggled with the prospect of women being preachers. As time went on, she got married and had six children. Unfortunately, five of those children died of diseases and Maria herself was struck with sickness. Being bedridden and unable to understand the horrific events unfolding she cried unto the Lord. As she began to submit herself to the Holy Spirit, he visited her in dreams. One night, she had a dream that she saw herself preaching the gospel to sinners and they turned to Jesus. She started to search the Scripture and came across women in the Bible being used by God. In the Bible, she saw women were ministers, evangelist, prophets, missionaries and had other leading roles and preached the gospel. These women were not silent, but they spared not to lift up their voices unto a dying world of sin. After many years of resisting the call, Maria finally submitted to the voice of God.

As she went out to preach in churches and her community people were weeping and getting saved, and her faith grew stronger to reach out to souls. Signs and wonders started to follow her as she began to step out into the deep. Thousands attended the miracle crusades that she could no longer keep up with the invitation to preach. At a meeting in the state of Ohio, God moved profoundly in her ministry as people started to fall out on the floor in a trance-like state. From that time and moving forward she was called the "trance evangelist" because people were falling under the power of God in her meetings (Warner). Thousands were crying and weeping for mercy and repenting as the fire of the Holy Ghost fell. She drew attention from newspapers and other churches as they came to see what was taking place in these meetings.

The convicting power of God was evident in her life and her ministry, as she submitted herself to the Pentecostal movement that swept the nation. She once said, "This is not new but God is giving the church back something it has lost".

At 74 years old after many years of ministry and thousands of miracles, Maria built a church near her home called "The Tabernacle" that seated five hundred (500) people. Today the church is still in existence and is affiliated with Assemblies of God under the name Lakeview Temple in Indianapolis (Warner). In the last 100 years, the church has grown to thousands of congregants, constructed 49 church buildings worldwide and 5 Bible schools.

In the 21st century, we continue to see the fruit of her work through the growth of Lakeview. The same healing anointing flowed through men and women of God. She paved the way for many as she was among the first to administer healing revival crusades. From Africa to America as the Lord multiplied the gift of healing and touching lives, people continue to fall under the power of God.

CATHERINE BOOTH
"And we find from Church history that the primitive Christians thus understood it; for that women did actually speak and preach amongst them we have indisputable proof." – Catherine Booth (Coutts.)

Raised a Methodist in a small town in England, Catherine was serious about God from an early age. At the age of 16, she became very sick and could not make it out of bed. It was at that time she began to write articles about the consumption of alcohol and the adverse effects. She also started reading the writings of John Wesley and Charles Finney who were the founders of the Methodist movement. These writings moved her faith, and as a result, she began to get a glimpse of her calling from God (Coutts).

From the beginning, Catherine was very firm in her belief in God and carried a burden for souls. She was a no-nonsense holiness woman that put God first. After a time, she met William Booth who would become her husband. They both shared an enormous burden for lost souls; however, he did not believe in women preaching. She went in search of the scriptures to convince him that God said in his word that he would pour out his spirit upon all flesh, but he still struggled with the thought. She kept feeling a stir in her spirit to speak God's word. One day while the service was in session Catherine walked up the aisle and ask her husband to allow her to speak (Coutts).

As she spoke the power of God came down, and everyone in the room including her husband was amazed at how eloquent her speech was and how she could expound on the word with such power. After that service, William became a supporter and a believer in women preaching the gospel. Catherine became a public speaker and preached the gospel with conviction, and many came to know the Lord. She believed in women ministering the gospel and through her organization the Salvation Army women were made leaders. When a woman by the name of Phoebe Palmer whom she highly regarded came under criticism for preaching the gospel, Catherine answered the critics with a thirty-page-pamphlet called Female Ministry/Women Right to preach the gospel - she wrote:

The Holy Spirit had been given to both sexes, Women had prophesied in the early church, and Paul's command to "keep silent" referred not to preaching but to gossip, interruption, and uncalled-for questions. "A mistaken application of the passage 'Let your women keep silent in the churches' has resulted in loss to the church, evil to the world, and dishonor to God." (Coutts).

Touched in his heart by the poor, her husband found his purpose as he walked the streets of England and saw many lost souls. He took the opportunity to reach out to the lost when the establishment had forgotten them both physically and spiritually. Being grieved in

NINETEENTH CENTURY FIRE WOMEN

their spirit they started to reach out to the alcoholics, prostitutes, and everyone that was left out by the political and the religious realm. In 1865, the Salvation Army was birthed, and the motto was blood and fire. Blood, which stood for the blood of Jesus, and fire for the presence of the Holy Spirit. The converts quickly became an army that marched around England and across the globe with the blood of Jesus and the fire of God in their mouth. In a short time, those who were once forsaken by the elite were touching thousands, as they walked through the dangerous street of England with the gospel.

This revival was so powerful as men and women were equally sharing the word of God; this was unheard of by the establishment of their time. Catherine stood with urgency and would not relent concerning the call to save souls. She was influential in challenging those that were outcast by the system to rise with a higher calling to preach this gospel. She made a case for the urgency of the gospel and shook the earth.

This movement opened the door for women to preach the gospel across the world. The Salvation Army is still marching with branches all over the world. They have equipped, taught and commissioned thousands to reach the lost and distributed food, shelter, clothing to millions around the world.

PANDITA RAMABAI

"I knew full well that it would displease my friends and my countrymen very much, but I have never regretted having taken the step. I was hungry for something better than the Hindu Sastras gave. I found it in the Christian Bible and was satisfied" -Pandita Ramabai (Minot 211).

The Hindu Religion could not satisfy her thirst or fill her empty spirit. She soon discovered the gift of God was free to all that believe in his son; and, annual pilgrimages and making payments, in her former religion, could never give true salvation. Her discovery led to one of greatest revival which took place in the "Mukti Mission" in the early 20th century.

Pandita Ramabai Saraswati was born on April 23, 1858, to the Sanskrit scholar Anant Shastri Dongre and Lakshmibai Dongre in India (Minot). She spent her childhood journey with her father that took her to pilgrimages across India in search of God. Restless and confused with her findings, Ramabai started to lose faith in Hinduism. Although a woman, Ramabai learned to read and write Sanskrit through her father, which was not traditionally taught to women. Through the influence of her scholarly father, Ramabai became known among the elite because of her ability to read Sanskrit text (a sacred language which is used by Hindus for worship in the Hindu temple). Because of her vast knowledge of literature, scholars called her Pandita, meaning "learned." She was the first woman to earn such a title.

Her recognition earned her a scholarship to England. In England, she was converted to Christianity. Ramabai was burdened with the predicament of Hindu women. She was saddened by the many young girls that were taken into marriage by older men; many of them became widows as their husbands died. Being widows, the majority of these young girls were left in the streets with no support.

In 1889, Ramabai returned to India and established the "Mukti Mission" which is an asylum for orphans and young widows. Her work quickly shifted from a religiously 'neutral' charity to an Evangelical Christian organization.

The sound of revival coming from Australia and Wales moved Ramabai to seek the Lord and also experience a revival in India. In 1905 through the leading of the Holy Spirit Ramabai gathered a group together to pray for revival for Indian Christians. A prayer group started with about 70 girls who committed to seeking God. Thus, revival fire began to flow through the mission. As the prayer group grew to about 500, powerful manifestations started to occur at the mission including speaking in tongues, prophecies, and visions.

The revival was marked by an intense hunger for righteousness, with cries for personal cleansing and sanctification. The young girls were so moved by the revival that they would spread the gospel among their neighbors, and even to other villages (Duewel). Many unusual manifestations occurred in the revival: visible tongues of fire, visions of Jesus, angelic visitations, dreams, shaking, and dancing before the Lord (McGee). There were also reports of joyful laughter, miraculous provisions of food, and young people prophesying.

At about this time, while the girls were praying early in the morning an appearance of flames surrounded one of the girl's body. One of the girls ran for a bucket of water but then realized that it was not literal fire. Later, through the testimony of the "inflamed" girl, passionate prayer and worship broke out in the school (Duewel). The school was lit with revival. In one service for over 24 hours the congregants cried out to God in prayer (Shaw).

The revival fire continued to burn for two years. In 1905, the baptism of the Holy Spirit came with the evidence of speaking in tongues. There were reports that several of the ladies at the mission would fluently speak English as the Spirit gave them utterance; these are native Indian women that neither spoke nor understood English (Shaw).

The revival continued along with the Pentecostal movement that was concurrently moving across the earth. Evangelist Ramabai was an educated woman of revival who advocated for social reform for women in India and became a catalyst of Pentecostal fire.

She received many awards because of her work in providing hope to widows, orphans, and the women of India. The British Monarchy awarded her the Kaisar-i-Hind Medal in 1919 (Shaw). In 1989, the Indian government recognized her contributions to the furtherance of Indian women (Shaw).

LUCY FARROW

Unrecognized but chosen by the Holy Spirit. Her determination to have a voice in the midst of prejudice, racism and injustice grew stronger as she carried the message of Pentecostalism in the late nineteenth to the early twentieth century. Born in the South as a slave her life was tough. She was among the elite of the Asuza Street Pentecostal movement. God through his grace allowed an upright vessel to use to show his glory. She received the gift of the Spirit, speaking in tongues and empowered many beyond race as Blacks, Whites, Hispanics, Asians and many others sought after the gift of the Holy Spirit. The power of God was released from heaven and flooded the streets from Los Angeles to New York as Lucy Farrow laid hands, and the fire of God fell from heaven.

Lucy decided to move to Texas where she pastored a small holiness congregation. It was at that time she made a divine connection with William Seymour who attended her church. Not long after, she met a man by the name of Charles Parham who was a teacher that came to town to hold meetings about the baptism of the Holy Spirit with the evidence of speaking in tongues. He explained that Christians could receive the baptism of the Holy Spirit just like the day of Pentecost. He went on to explain that at his Bible College many of the students were filled with the Holy Spirit and spoke in other tongues. Parham was drawn to Lucy, and he and his wife invited her to be their governess (Hyatt).

She left Texas and headed to Baxter Spring with the Parham's and left the church in the hands of Seymour to pastor. While staying at the Parham's house, Lucy got filled with the Holy Spirit and spoke in tongues. At some point, she returned to Texas and told the church about her experience. Being a woman of humility, she influenced Seymour to attend Bible college. Seymour attended Bible college for a while and then headed to Los Angeles where he met others and started teaching about the baptism of the Holy Spirit. In Los Angeles Seymour told the story of Farrow and her gift of laying hands to receive the baptism of the Holy Spirit. They were anxious to have her join them in Los Angeles. At her arrival, she remained in the house of Mr. Lee who hosted her. As he came through the door and saw Farrow, he started to plead with her to lay hands on him to receive the baptism of the Holy Spirit which she replied: "I cannot do it unless the Lord say so" (Hyatt).

That same evening while at the dinner table Farrow rose up from her seat and looked at Lee in the eyes and said, "The Lord tells me to lay my hands on you for the Holy Ghost" (Hyatt). After she laid hands on Lee, he fell to the floor and immediately started to speak in tongues.

Shortly after they attended a prayer meeting, which was being held by a couple that lived in a house on Bonnie Brae Street. At the prayer meeting, many started to be filled with Holy Spirit, speaking in other tongues. Not too long after that, people started to come to the house from across the country to receive or to witness the manifestation of the Spirit.

Farrow went on to minister across the USA and England where there were manifestations of the Holy Spirit, and many fell under the power of God. The Lord released his anointing upon her life, and many received various gifts through her laying of hands. Afterward, she went to Africa where she persuaded a tribe to accept the Lord Jesus Christ. Reportedly, through the manifestation of the Holy Spirit, she supernaturally spoke their language, and they were able to receive salvation and the baptism of the Holy Spirit.

Although her name is not well known, Lucy Farrow caused a stir in the realm of the Spirit, and a movement was birthed. She was a crucial element in the fastest growing movement known to humanity. Millions manifested the baptism of the Holy Spirit through speaking in tongues. Thousands of Churches took hold of the practice and by doing so the gift of healing, miracles, preaching and teachings were poured out to all that sought after it. Today the Pentecostal-charismatic movement has reached all continents, nations, and tongues.

TWENTIETH CENTURY WOMEN OF REVIVAL

AIMEE MCPHERSON

"I ponder and pray in the stillness, I dream as a dreamer of dreams. A steepled church stands before me — a church with open doors. Within it I see the preacher stand; hear his voice in earnest call. But 'tis the throng that flows through the street outside that holds my anxious gaze." – Aimee Semple McPherson (McPherson 670).

IN A TIME when women did not have many rights, God rose up Aimee McPherson to preach the gospel. Unfamiliar with women preachers in her days, some found her interesting as she publicly dramatized stories of the Bible to get the attention of the people in the streets of the town. She shattered the culture of her time and became a powerful force that triggered a change in the Christian world.

The founder of the Foursquare Gospel Church, Evangelist Aimee McPherson was an effective speaker, mesmerizing the crowd with her ability to deliver the message of the cross. Born in Canada in 1890 to a mother who was a minister at the Salvation Army, Aimee had a desire to know who God was for herself. While in school she was taught that God did not exist but within her soul she desired to have a personal relationship with God. One day she began to cry out to

God asking Him to show himself to her and He showed up, and she received salvation.

At the age of 17, she went to a Pentecostal service that changed her spiritual life as she heard people crying out to God and speaking in tongues; she was moved by what she saw. Aimee converted to Pentecostalism and got married to the minister Robert Semple who preached at that service. He took it upon himself to mentor and disciple her concerning a spiritual lifestyle in Christ. Shortly after, they went to China on a mission trip where he fell sick and died ("Aimee Semple McPherson Biography"). Being a young widow and pregnant Aimee returned home. In a time when women had little rights, Aimee settled for regular life, raising a child on her own. As time went by, she got ill. Reports claimed that she died on the operating table and came back to life. While on the dying bed, she later recalled the story of hearing a voice say "now will you go" she gladly answered, "yes Lord" (McPherson 76). She was miraculously healed of her sickness and left the hospital with a newfound mission.

Burdened for souls, she drove across the country in a car that was called "the gospel car" preaching from Canada to the states of America. The Pentecostal fire was so much within her bones that anywhere her feet touched whether in the rain, snow or heat Aimee McPherson was out in the street captivating the hearts of the lost with the gospel of Jesus Christ. Within her pursuit for souls to be saved, she grew in popularity and also in fame. Her power-packed, tongue-speaking, devil tormenting meetings brought many to know Jesus Christ as their Lord and Savior. She went on to preach in fully packed auditoriums and churches across the country; the crowds would come from early morning until late at night. Once she told the story of finding a man hiding inside the bathroom of the church in the night so that he can be in the meetings for the morning.

One night as she sought the Lord in prayer God spoke to her and said He would give her Los Angeles. She quickly responded and headed to Los Angeles and preached the gospel in every corner of the city. Shortly after, she built a church called Angeles Temple that held about 5,000 people. The glory of God fell in the building, and a revival broke forth in Los Angeles. The sick were laid out on stretchers inside the church; many in the hospital booked ambulances to bring them to the meetings so they could get healed. The lines stretched a mile long as the crowds patiently waited for prayer. She also had one of the most well-known radio stations in Los Angeles with thousands of listeners. Her fame went abroad as she traveled to numerous countries and preached the gospel. She was indeed a yielded vessel as the Lord opened the door for media, and radio programs. She published books, magazines and was known and recognized by the prominent figures of her time.

As a pastor, she led and oversaw workers, ministers and other pastors that worked under her leadership. She also helped to grow the ministry of local church pastors in Los Angeles. Despite her effort to merge with the Assemblies of God, she was consistently denied, and so she formed a new denomination. She is the founder of Life Pacific College that was started in 1923 as McPherson had a desire to equip men and women of God to become Missionaries, Evangelist, and Pastors. After the opening of the Angeles Temple, which was the first branch, other branches followed in Pasadena, Santa Monica, and Santa Ana. Today all four churches are still active with branches in all 50 states and different parts of the world.

KATHRYN KUHLMAN

"The world called me a fool for having given my entire life to One whom I've never seen. I know exactly what I'm going to say when I stand in His presence. When I look upon that wonderful face of Jesus, I'll have just one thing to say: 'I tried.' I gave of myself the best I knew how. My redemption will have been perfected when I stand and see Him who made it all possible" – *Kathryn Kuhlman (Liardon).*

Kathryn Kuhlman was a mighty woman of God who God raised up in a time when American culture began to glorify sex, drugs, and money. American society started to take a back seat concerning the gospel, and many wanted to live their lives as they chose. In the countryside was a young girl who was captivated by the heart of God.

Accustomed to the religious customs of her town, a young Kathryn Kuhlman went to the altar just like many times before. This time it was different as a guest minister was conducting two weeks of revival meetings at her church. While at the altar on that Sunday morning, Kathryn was touched by the Holy Spirit and began to cry uncontrollably. From that day she was born again and sanctified. Her life was forever transformed. All of her church friends, adults included failed to understand what happened to her as tears ran down her face. The fourteen-year-old Kathryn had a close encounter with the Lord. She no longer had a mere religious relationship with God, but she had now entered His presence. And within His presence, she would shake the religious and cultural walls of her time.

Born and raised in Concordia, Missouri, Kathryn was brought up in the church with parents that were firm believers. At the age of 16, Kathryn's sister convinced their mother to allow Kathryn to travel. Her mother agreed, and this was the start of Kathryn's ministry.

The establishment of her 'miracle services' started in 1946 when a young woman was healed of a tumor through her ministry (Smith). This was the start of a phenomenon as the Lord would give her words of knowledge to call out direct disorders and illnesses in the crowd. Many received their healing. Many would fall under the power of God as she ministered: cancers were removed; eyes were opened, and the lame walked just like in the Bible days. Healing and salvation through Christ touched all who came to her meetings. She was able to cross denominational lines and broke the ceiling glass by ministering and healing millions.

For over a decade Kathryn Kuhlman would pack out the Los Angeles Auditorium with 7,000 people per meeting. She expanded into radio and television producing more than 500 telecasts. She ministered in churches, halls, tents, and auditoriums that seated thousands. Kathryn became a national sensation, and she was not ashamed to speak about the Holy Spirit. Her sensitivity and teachings caused a generation of church leaders to relearn about the power of the Holy Spirit and submit their ministry to the understanding that the Holy Spirit is a person.

Today many still read her books and listen to her messages. She is credited with influencing thousands of ministries worldwide that believe in the healing movement through the power of the Holy Spirit.

PRESENT DAY WOMEN OF REVIVAL

WITHIN THIS SECTION of the book, we present the ministry of women who began in the twentieth century but continues to this day. These are women who have walked in the power of the Holy Spirit and have been used by God to win many souls worldwide, and or to ignite revival. As these women are still alive, presenting them in this book is not an endorsement of all their activities, but instead an acknowledgement that they are women that were used by God to win souls and impact the body of Christ.

The first two women Carmelita Collins, and Euphema Collins, although not as well-known as some of the other women, are included because they were instrumental in the rise of the Harvest Army World Revival Movement currently impacting the world through Worldwide Vision Day. They continue in the line of women of revival whom God has used to win many souls and impact the body of Christ.

CARMELITA COLLINS
"If I could rip the heart of man and put salvation inside of them I would do it" – Mama Collins.

While men slept across the island of Jamaica, the travailing voice of Carmelita Collins could be heard in prayer by men and by God.

Every morning before the sun rose, Mama Collins, as she was often called, could be found on her knees making supplications to God for the church, community, country, and particularly unbelievers. Her heart mourned and ached as she read the scriptures regarding man's destination if they do not repent of their wicked ways and turn to a loving God. It is with that bleeding heart that she drew strength to pray. She may not have recognized it in the beginning, but through the seed of prayer, God birthed one of the most impactful street ministries in modern day history.

Mama Collins is a dynamic woman of God with an unusual anointing for street ministry. Her ability to pray and divinely connect to the throne of God caused great and troubled men to seek her. She preached the gospel wailing like a woman in pain as she cried for the souls of men as if it was the last call.

In her early years as a Christian, Mama Collins attended a Baptist church. While participating in the formal Baptist services, the Holy Spirit would move upon her, and she would praise God with a loud voice. She would sing and worship in the spirit. However, the church felt that her praise and worship were only distractions in the service. One day, being annoyed, a woman walked up and hit her on the back with a Bible as an indication that she was too loud in the service. She loved the church but overwhelmed by the Spirit of God she found a home at the New Testament Church of God in Falmouth, Trelawny. As a result of her faithfulness, she became a Sunday school teacher, and then the president of the ladies' ministry. She progressed and became the district president of the ladies' ministry, and also ran various office duties. In spite of the activities and positions in the church, Mama Collins continued to experience what she calls a "heavy duty call " upon her life.

One day, Mama Collins fell into a trance for three days where she was not able to move, eat, drink or remember anything that was happening in the natural state of mind. As she laid there, others kept a record of what she was saying as she was receiving visions from God. After three days she regained natural consciousness, and God spoke to her and said: "You are called for street ministry." From that time she willingly submitted to the call of God.

A Woman Street Soldier is Born.

The streets of Jamaica were never the same as this fierce and thunderous preacher went from town to town and city to city with the fire of God in her mouth. She could be heard in the square of Falmouth quoting the Bible and salvation verses such as John 3:16 *"For God so love the world that he gave his only begotten son for whosoever believe in him shall not perish but have everlasting life."*

Many gazed in amazement as souls cried out for salvation through a little woman in the square of Falmouth. Word spread throughout the community that a woman was preaching the gospel with tears in her eyes, compassion in her heart, and prayer on her lips. The result was staggering as God gave evidence of her calling through many receiving Christ in their life.

As news of her preaching continued to spread, the leaders of her church were not happy with the work that she was doing. Because of her various roles in the church including being president of the ladies' ministry, the leadership of the church called her in for disciplinary action. With seven men in the room Mama Collins was interrogated and accused of insubordination. As the men stood and looked toward her, they requested that she answer to the charges against her. The Holy Spirit came upon her, and she humbly spoke the following words to the men:

"With due respect Sirs! If this thing be of man, it will vanish away, but if it be of God, it will stand. Take heed sirs lest you think you're fighting against me you're fighting against God...The Lord has anointed me to go on the streets."

Her response pierced the air and silenced the men. She later stated that during those times some thought that she was losing her mind, but she remained bold-faced and focused on the call in her life. Mama Collins continued to preach on the street corners, at the police stations, hospitals, prisons, supermarkets, outdoor markets, city and town squares. She was often seen riding her bike which she calls her "mission bike" while young men would push a makeshift wheeled cart to preach the gospel. The cart attracted many because of the music that was playing as she witnessed to every soul. God continued to use her ministry as souls came to Christ in every street, square, district, and parish where she preached. She was invited to conduct revivals in many churches across Jamaica. Tens of thousands of souls came to Jesus.

In the midst of the Lord moving in her life, there were also trials as many challenged the anointing that God placed in her life. One day, a Rastafarian man rose up against her as she preached the gospel. He started to spew many offensive words, but he was mostly enraged that a woman was boldly preaching in the public square. He began to place demands on her and ordered her to stay silent. As he approached her with rage and force, her life seemingly at risk, she shouted, "The blood of Jesus is against you." Shortly after, he died, which grieved her greatly.

On another occasion, a thief broke into her home in the night. He tied her up, pulled out a gun and ordered her to give him her money. With his hands on the trigger, he proceeded to urge the woman of God to submit to his order. She looked into his eyes and with the fire of God said to him "in the name of Jesus you cannot shoot me." He started to shake and tried to pull the trigger! She spoke a second time again "in the name of Jesus you cannot shoot me." Angered by her boldness, he tried to pull the trigger a third time. She again warned him and said, "In the name of Jesus you cannot shoot me." Uncontrollably, the man continued to shake as the gun fell out of his hands and he took flight into the night. She was fearless when it came to preaching the gospel, and the anointing that God placed in her life started to be recognized.

Mama Collins' prayers were packed with the power of the Holy Spirit as she raised her voice unto the Lord for mercy, grace, and salvation for the lost. Her heart was opened to the leaders in her community as they sought after her to lead them in prayer. On a weekly basis, she was invited to pray with school leaders and police officers for guidance, safety, and protection. Her impact went beyond her community as influential men and women from the political, business and religious realm received counsel from Mama Collins. She never turned away anyone that sought advice whether they came publicly or privately. Mama Collins always remained focused on reaching out to lost souls. Her ministry continued to take root as she preached in some of the largest churches in Jamaica. She ran crusades in every parish across the country and ministered in tent meetings. The Lord also allowed her to travel to the USA, Bahamas, and Grand Cayman.

Throughout the years Mama Collins has been a hospitable woman of God. She provided housing for young men and women, and the Lord used her to raise them up as preachers. It is reported that *"there is not a man or woman that came through her house that has not been charged under God with the ministry."* Through raising up many pastors, missionaries, and evangelists, an estimated one hundred thousand souls have been reached through her ministry. The impact of her ministry is felt across the world through men and women of God that were mentored by her to carry the same mantle that God has placed upon her life. She is a pioneer in her own right as she set the foundational tone for the Harvest Army Church International in Jamaica.

Mama Collins has achieved several awards and recognition from several entities. This includes a honorary award from the Mayor of Falmouth, Jamaica, and the local Police Department. The hospital in which she worked for 26 years also recognized her tremendous accomplishments in the ministry.

At the age of 87, Mama Collins showed no signs of slowing down. She continues to minister in prayer to many leaders who now visit her home from time to time. She remains passionate and continues to mentor, disciple, and counsel the young people. At about the turn of the century, Mama Collins was encouraged by her son to get her driving license and to put the "mission bike" in retirement. Although she was reluctant, despite her age, she passed the driving test without any error. Mama Collins could now be seen driving her car around town with a blow horn installed on top preaching the gospel. She remains an inspiration to women across the world who hear the call of God. God wants you to break through the barriers and fulfill the call of God in your life.

EUPHEMA COLLINS
"Born to Bear and on Fire"

"What of the night? What of the night?" She cried, as her voice became like a trumpet - a woman in travail for the restoration of the city, tears running down her face in pain and agony for the dying souls. A young convert looked on in great awe as the Evangelist preached Isaiah 21:11 which asked the question "Watchman what of the night?" As the preacher continued to speak, the church thundered with the wailing of the saints and the urgency of the word came upon the people. Many cried aloud, spoke in tongues and uttered prophetic warnings to the city. That night the life of a young convert was changed forever as the burden for souls was birthed.

Like Priscilla with Aquila of the Acts of the Apostles, God has raised up Apostle Dr. E.E. Collins to mobilize and train hundreds of ministers of the Gospel worldwide who had never preached on the streets. Today many of their churches have exploded in dramatic growth because these leaders then trained their colleagues and laymen to do the same.

As she entered many countries, she witnessed, preached on the streets and trained congregations to do the same thing. In one case while in Lesotho, Africa, she trained believers at a mid-day gathering of the churches in the capital city. After the training, she immediately dispatched them to the center of the town. Hundreds of attendees abandoned their belongings and stormed the city preaching the gospel. She repeats this in many other countries where she goes. Imagine thousands of believers mobilized to witness and preach. Imagine the tens of thousands saved from the ministry of these recruits. Even in India, Sri Lanka and other Eastern countries, where it is not customary, she was able to raise up women to preach with power.

Apostle Collins was born in Jamaica, West Indies. She received Christ at the age of thirteen (13), and was filled with the Holy Spirit shortly after. From that time she felt the hand of God upon her life. She asked the Lord about the purpose of the infilling and mighty anointing upon her life. She found it in the Word of God in Acts 1:8 *"But ye shall receive power, after that the Holy Ghost is come upon you: and ye shall be witnesses unto me both in Jerusalem, and in all Judaea, and in Samaria, and unto the uttermost part of the earth."* Before graduating from high school, she inquired about Bible college in her church body, but at that time women were not trained as ministers. She continued her strong soul-winning ministry but opted for business college. By age 23, she married Keith Collins, the director of evangelism at her church and leader of a gospel band. After having her first child, they migrated to Florida where her husband studied at Miami Christian College. Shortly after that, a second child was born into the family.

In Miami this young evangelist was particularly very intensive and compelling in her outreach as many street preachers, transit preachers who had stopped, resumed after meeting her. As people got saved, they would be sent to local churches. Sometimes after, they would meet some of them who had backslidden. When asked what happened, many would say because they wanted to be pastored by her husband and her. By this time God had already visited them in a vision about planting churches and the inauguration of a worldwide church body.

In 1990, Euphema Collins co-founded the inauguration of Harvest Army Church in Miami. She led nearly every service and conducted daily personal evangelism. Thousands came to Jesus. Most of them went to established churches, but some stayed at the new church. Many healings and miracles took place as they went from house to house. While witnessing at a home, a lady was invited to their service after receiving Christ. She said she could not because she had not walked for two (2) years. She was told, "Since that is your hindrance, rise up and walk, in Jesus' name." She shockingly surprised herself and began to walk. The explosion from that reverberated so strongly that by Sunday, her entire family and clan came to church and received Christ.

In her preaching, she once told the story of how God spoke while she was on a bus and told her to move from her seat. Without fully understanding what was happening she submitted unto the Lord. Shortly after, there was an accident on the bus, and someone else that took that seat was severely damaged.

By 1992, she moved to New York with her husband and planted more Harvest Army churches. The church planting spread to Jamaica. She enrolled in seminary and pursued her education until she had achieved a B.A. and M.A. in Pastoral Ministry and a Ph.D. in Social Science. She has authored a book on discipleship called "Soul Survival" and another on the Holy Spirit called "Fire on the Mountain." She is the chancellor for Harvest Army International Seminary where she also lectures intermittently.

It was evident that the Lord prepared Apostle Collins to listen to his voice and ignites the Spirit of prophecy. She is also much admired for her ability to show compassion and honored for her spirit to fight for the saints in prayer.

The following is a story of a female minister, a woman, that knows all too well the power of a praying pastor.

A young couple had a son, and for ten years they tried to have more children but were unsuccessful. One day as the preaching went forth the preacher gave a prophetic word. "Someone in here wants to have a child, and the Lord wants to give you the baby." Although she was afraid she went forth to receive the prayer from Apostle E. E. Collins. Within a month she discovered that she was pregnant and was overjoyed with the fact that after ten (10) years of waiting God had finally answered her.

Within the same time frame, she received another call from another young minister that her doctor said that a medical test revealed that the child in her womb had a hole in the heart and may not live much longer. With a shaky voice and tears rolling down her face she called Apostle E.E. Collins and explained to her what the doctor had said. Without fear and her faith unshaken, Apostle Collins prayed a prayer of deliverance over the young minister. That night, the young minister reportedly slept with the peace of God within her knowing that it was in the Lord's hands. Soon after that, she was sent to do more testing. The nurse approached her and said, "What are you here for?" At that point, the minister smiled, and she said well, "I am here because the doctor said..." Before she could finish her sentence, the nurse said: "Go home, there is nothing wrong with your baby." God received the glory because a woman of God opened her heart to pray.

Moreover, the ministry of Apostle E. E. Collins has had a powerful impact on women across the world. Her sermon "Rise Up Ye Women" from Isaiah 32 is remembered in many countries especially in India, Philippines, and Central America. Around the world, many women have become missionaries, evangelists, pastors, and overseers. After several revelations from the Lord concerning world evangelism, Senior Apostle Collins was seen as the spiritual womb as she rose up mightily to execute 'THE GREAT GATHERING'. Since 2003, The Great Gathering has been a gathering of churches from across the world for 21 days in New York. She has also been the spiritual womb for the revelation of 'GOD'S REVIVAL' since 2007, which advocates that every believer is a preacher. Furthermore, the mighty revelation of 'WORLDWIDE VISION DAY' since 2014 in which the body of Christ worldwide is mobilized to do personal evangelism and street preaching on the first Saturday of every 3 months; and, 'DAILY REVIVAL' since 2018 where believers worldwide are called to preach virtually every day for 3½ years like Jesus did. Imagine the womb for these mighty soul-saving revelations. By the publishing of this book, almost every country in the world had been touched by her ministry with many receiving Christ.

As she enters a country, the apostolic office starts to operate as God uses her to ignite the fire to preach the gospel in many churches. Her book "Fire on the Mountaintop" has done much to augment this explosion. The anointing and fire on her life are released in the churches as men and women fall under the power of God, speak in tongues, and God fills their lives with the burden of winning the lost.

After the Corona Pandemic struck the earth in 2020, Apostle Collins was hindered from continuing her ministry travels to her intended 200 countries. She turned her sight on fulfilling a commission to her church called 'Church Planting Revolution'. By 2021, she was visiting Florida USA quite often and had spearheaded new churches in Orlando, Tampa, Pine Hills, Kissimmee and Palm Bay. She was found very gifted in acquiring suitable buildings for new churches. Many souls turned to the Lord.

For over twenty-five (25) years Apostle E.E. Collins has been seen on international television, sometimes along with her husband with viewership numbering over 100 million households on many international networks including 'The Word Network' and many national and local networks. She has ministered in more than seventy (70) countries, on the streets, in churches with a handful of people or to more than 50,000 at once, while millions view or listen live by radio or television. More than 250,000 people are estimated to have received Christ through her ministry directly and indirectly.

MARILYN HICKEY

"I said 'Lord I am a woman,' but he replied, "that is not your problem. "That is my problem. Your problem is to have faith".-Marilyn Hickey (Hagberg 42)

Marilyn Hickey defies the odds in the Muslim dominated world where she is honored and embraced with open arms as she preached the message of hope in Jesus Christ. Having ripped through the veil of the Muslim strongholds at the age of 87 years old, Marilyn Hickey shows no sign of retiring. The older she gets, the more the crowds grow, and souls are getting saved. Within 40 years of ministry, Marilyn Hickey has been to 136 countries. She is a New York Times bestseller, and she is also the first woman to join the Board of Directors of the largest church in the world.

Born on July 1, 1931, in Dalhart, Texas Marilyn Hickey was raised as a Methodist. At a young age, Hickey saw first-hand as mental illness took over her family. At the of 11, Marilyn was told by doctors that she had an enlarged heart and needed medical intervention to live. As a teen, she realized that God had a plan for her life and she became a born-again Christian. Growing up Marilyn's desire was to be a language teacher and eventually go into international politics, but God intervened because her call was to speak the language of the Holy Spirit to a dying world.

After many years, Marilyn started to attend the Assemblies of God where she met her husband Wallace Hickey, who also served as a pastor. Though she did not have any experience, she was obedient to the call of God. Marilyn and her husband started to preach the gospel by driving in a car and doing tent meeting revivals. Soon after the couple was pastoring a small Assemblies of God church and Marilyn was doing door to door ministry where she developed a love for teaching the Bible. In 1960, they moved to Denver, Colorado where they started the full Gospel Church which eventually became Orchard Road Christian

Center. When Hickey and her husband started the church, they had 25 members. By the mid-80s it grew to over two thousand (2000) members (Hagberg). Today the church is one of the largest churches in Denver, Colorado.

At the age of 42, The Lord spoke to Marilyn and said it was time for her to move to a higher level. God continued speaking to her and said: "I want you to cover the earth with the word" (Hagberg 42). Marilyn replied and told God she was just a woman. Not only was she a woman but also, she was not a pulpit preacher, she was a Sunday school teacher that found joy in teaching others the word of God. God answered Hickey and said: you being a woman is "*not your problem it is my problem; your problem is to have faith*" (Hagberg 42). Her eyes became open to the truth, and that is God uses anyone that is yielded to his word. She submitted to God's will from that day forward. After that experience with God, Hickey started teaching the Bible in 22 homes and the crowds grew rapidly. Within a short time, thousands attended these studies and soon after her students were requesting for her to begin a radio broadcast (Draper).

Denver, Colorado was not big enough for what God had in store for Hickey. Reaching thousands through radios and broadcasting was tremendous, but God was just getting started. Although she did not initially know it, her calling was global. One day Marilyn saw a story in the newspaper that transformed her ministry forever. In 1983 Hickey read a story about Ethiopia that brought her ministry to a turning point. Ethiopia was stricken with famine and disease, and thousands were dying including children. Hickey was heartbroken as she decided to travel to Ethiopia with aid for the people.

The government of Ethiopia welcomed the physical help for their people, but Hickey had something else in mind. She came to lay hands on the sick and the dying and to show forth the power of Jesus Christ to a dying world. They would not allow her to pray or to hold any meetings with the people because they were Muslims. At that time, she left

Ethiopia disappointed as she went back to America. However, in 2002 a couple of years after that incident Marilyn went back into Ethiopia and hosted a healing meeting that brought 40,000 people to the Lord (Hagberg 43). This meeting was the start of her journey to preach the gospel in many dangerous countries. Many male preachers would not dare to enter some of these countries with the gospel, but God sent a little woman.

Marilyn went into consistent prayer for the countries of the world. She wrote down the name of every nation, and daily would be in prayer for each one. But as Hickey prayed, God would press on her concerning the Muslim countries, especially Pakistan. Many thought that she was insane as she embarked in a new and dangerous mission to save souls in the Muslim countries especially in Pakistan. Pakistan is on the terrorist list of the USA where top Islamic terrorists are known to hide, but Hickey defies the odds that are against her gender by winning tens of thousands of souls in that dangerous country.

In 1995 through prayer, God revealed to her that she must go into the Muslim territories especially Pakistan. Hickey went and took her first trip to Pakistan in Lahore and held a healing meeting that attracted thousands of people. Those that believe received deliverance instantaneously from all manner of sicknesses and demonic possession as she preached the word of God. Signs and wonders followed so strong in a country where a majority of the population does not believe Jesus is the Son of God, much less that a woman can be used to bring restoration.

A man by the name of Anwar Fazal was among the thousands Hickey led to the Lord in those transforming meetings. Her mantle fell upon Fazal as God's purpose for his life became clear. Over the years he became known as the Billy Graham of Pakistan and his congregation seats 30,000. Although Pakistan is 96 percent Muslim, Fazal launched a Christian television network called Isaac TV that reached every home in Pakistan. His network has an enormous impact in spreading the gospel in the Muslim country. In 2016 Hickey took her seventh trip to Pakistan where she united with pastor Anwar Fazal, and he helped Hickey in hosting the largest event she ever had in Pakistan where more than one (1) million attended her meeting (Berglund).

God has anointed her feet to cross over dangerous territories. Hickey confessed that most times the radical Muslims left her alone because she was an "old, stupid, weak and harmless woman that is just talking foolishly." They saw her as no threat. However, she did receive threats from thirty (30) suicide bombers that threatened to kill her in her meetings. But these threats only worked to her advantage.

God also used her to impact Sudan with the gospel. She had a three-night crusade in Sudan with 37,000 attending on the first night, 45,000 the second night, 54,000 the following night, and 60,000 on the final night (Hagberg 43). There are reports of many who have received healings and miracles at the Sudan meetings.

She's been to China more than thirty (30) times ministering to Seminary students and Christians at government-approved churches. She's been to Pakistan numerous times. Other countries that her ministry has touched include Italy, Morocco, Ethiopia, Sudan, Russia, Egypt, Panama, Australia, Hungary, Germany, India, The United Kingdom, Vietnam, and dozens more.

Today Hickey is considered the "Mother of Pakistan" as many continue to flock to her meetings in a country where it should have been impossible (Berglund). Hickey's influence is intercultural, intergenerational and matriarchal in nations where women have to stay covered. She has met and prayed with high-ranking officials of many non-Christian countries, and they receive her graciously even protecting her as she expounds the word of God. Many have been martyred in these nations because they preached the gospel, but God has used Hickey to break through these barriers. Her lectures on healing and the Bible have broken records for the largest public meeting in Pakistan history; her teachings have had a similar impact in Cairo, Egypt, and other Muslim territories.

While many have retired while reflecting on memories of the past, hundreds of thousands remain transfixed on an eighty-seven (87) year old woman who tells them that Jesus saves.

Marilyn Hickey has traveled to more than 136 countries including places that are deemed unreachable and hard for many Christians (Brown and Patrick). She has published 110 books which have been translated into 27 languages. Her television program which started along with her daughter Sarah can be seen on over 130 countries with a potential audience of 2.2 billion households worldwide ("FAQ"). Her crowd breaking records across the world surpass some of the biggest names of our time.

JOYCE MEYER

She mesmerizes her audience with her humorous and straightforward teachings as she uses her struggles and victories to show others that they can overcome the world. She is well known for her charismatic personality and knack for practical Bible teaching. She seems to connect with every age group. Using her gifts, she wins thousands to the Lord.

Meyer is a charismatic Christian author, and conference speaker who is well known for her Bible teachings. No matter who comes in contact with her, Meyer always seems to find a way to captivate their attention. Her messages on hope and transformation have caused thousands to renew their purpose by refocusing on the word for full deliverance. Her messages have brought hope, courage, and strength to those that felt weakened by life circumstance.

She was born Pauline Joyce Hutchison in June 4, 1943 (Georgiou). Meyer got saved at the age of nine when she realized that she needed Jesus Christ to escape the dark world around her (Georgiou). At the age of 35 Meyer had an encounter with the Lord and she suddenly felt the presence of God flowing through her. She began leading at an early morning Bible class in Life Christian Bible Center which is located in St. Louis. Eventually Meyer became the church associate pastor. This promotion was due to her Bible teaching style that drew many to the church. She also began airing a 15-minute radio broadcast in her local town (Georgiou). In 1985 Joyce Meyer resigned from Life Christian Bible Center and started her own ministry called "Life In The Word". Her radio shows expanded to different states and her popularity reached across the states.

Today Joyce Meyer's ministry can be found on television as well as radio. Her popular TV and Radio program called Enjoying Everyday Life can be seen and heard by hundreds of radio stations and TV stations nationally and worldwide. In February 2005 Joyce Meyer was featured on the cover of Time Magazine as one of the influential Evangelicals in America (Time Staff). Meyer has written over 100 non-fictional books and produced TV, and radio programs in 90 languages and 200 countries (Meyer). Now in her mid-seventies her conferences continue to attract people that are looking for practicality through the word of God.

JUANITA BYNUM

God rose up Dr. Juanita Bynum in a time when the church world needed a female figure to stand against ungodliness in the body of Christ. Using her gifts from God and highlighting some of her failures, Bynum drew global attention. Her audience grew dramatically when she released her book "No More Sheets." She went into detail about how the enemy had her wrapped up and imprisoned her through sexual immorality and different strongholds that caused her life to spin out of control. Her testimony was intriguing as many flocked to hear her speak about how she overcame the trap of the enemy. She stood firm on the message of holiness and righteousness in a time when sexual sin permeated the church culture.

Growing up in Chicago with her parents and siblings, Bynum embraced the church as a fundamental part of her life. Her father was an elder in the church. According to Ministries Today she was an outgoing child. Her performance in her middle school's production grabbed the attention of television agents who wanted to cast her in programs. However, her mother declined the offers. "I used to make her stop playing outside and come in the house and just sit still," she told Ministries Today. "I wanted my daughter to listen to the voice of God."

Juanita Bynum preached her first sermon when she was 12 years old. Still a teenager, she began preaching at churches and revivals. At 16, she was invited to do a three-day revival. When she started ministering, there were about 20 people. By the time her father came to pick her up, the church was packed. From that time, she would begin to discover her calling as a mighty preacher. Realizing her growing impact Bynum released a series called 'Lessons on Submission'.

In 1997, Juanita Bynum released a video and audio series called 'No More Sheets'. In 1998, world re-known Bishop T.D. Jakes took notice of her message and the unusual anointing upon her life and booked her for a popular conference in the USA. She delivered a sermon titled "No More Sheets" to 52,000 attending women. This impacted the lives of many who would later listen to the message or read her book on the subject. Bynum told Essence "It wasn't me—it was God." More than a million video copies of "No More Sheets" were sold.

Bynum began to appear regularly on the then largest Christian television entity in USA and the world, Trinity Broadcasting Corporation, where she reportedly drew very large viewership. Other notable television networks included Daystar and The Word Network where she even had her own program.

According to AAE Speakers, Juanita Bynum is one of the most sought after 21st Century female speakers, teachers, lecturers and entrepreneurs. In 2014, she was awarded the Citizenship Award from the State of Georgia making her an ambassador for that state. In 2016, she received the President Obama Volunteer Award for her service to the community.

Bynum's impactful ministry spans across continents hosting standing room only crusades in Brazil, Dominican Republic, France, Ghana, Netherlands, South Africa, Swaziland, Uganda, United Kingdom, Zambia, and Zimbabwe among other countries. In January 2018, she was installed and inaugurated as an Ambassador to the United Nations. She received the honor of becoming the Goodwill Ambassador to Bayelsa State Nigeria.

Across continents she hosted standing room only crusades in Brazil, Dominican Republic, France, Ghana, Netherlands, South Africa, Swaziland, Uganda, United Kingdom, Zambia, and Zimbabwe among other countries.

Dr. Bynum has authored many Christian books that have been read by millions especially women seeking for deliverance and development in ministry. She is a platinum recording artist and New York Times Best Selling Author. In 2007, she released an album titled 'Piece of My Passion', and The New York Times described her as "the most prominent black female Television Evangelist in the country."

It was obvious that Bynum's rise on the ministry scene triggered the rise of many women who had been held back in ministry. Thousands of women preachers, Evangelists and Prophetesses, began to seek advance in their ministry. The observant attendee or viewer could easily see and hear the personality, tone and mannerism of Juanita Bynum in their delivery.

For a season she held major early morning prayer travail sessions that drew thousands of people from across the USA and worldwide to New York. In the nights she would preach and minister deliverance to thousands.

Several notable spiritual magazines have featured her on their cover including Charisma, Spirit Led Women, Ministries Today and others.

Juanita Bynum was clearly burdened with the plight of mankind and his soul as sometimes she could be heard on her Television program beckoning the Body of Christ to arise and join with Ministries emphasizing personal evangelism throughout the USA and worldwide. Her positive effect on tens of thousands of female preachers is undeniable. Millions have come to the Lord from her direct ministry and many more through those who have risen up ministry because of her example.

Indeed Dr. Bynum has helped and continues to help the nations as a soul saving woman of the 21st century.

HEIDI BAKER

Heidi Baker is known as "Mama Aida" in the country of Mozambique where thousands of children embrace her and follow her teaching of Christ. She oversees Bible schools, medical clinics, church-based orphan care, well drilling, primary schools, evangelistic industries, cottage farms, widow's programs, and healing outreaches in remote villages that includes a network of hundreds of churches. Heidi Baker earned her BA, and MA degrees from Vanguard University and her Ph.D. from Kings College, University of London (Baker). Heidi Baker's greatest passion is to see the glory and the presence of God manifested in the body of Christ and to care for the children whom she has won to Christ.

She and her husband Rolland Baker started to pour out their lives to the abandoned children and as result revival broke out. The children began to cry and weep for the presence of God and miracles, and healings started to take place. Soon after, the presence of God swept through the villages as pastors, churches, and adults from all ten provinces of Mozambique joined in the revival.

Heidi Baker was born on August 29, 1959. At the age of 16, Heidi received Jesus Christ in her life. Soon after she received a vision for several hours and the Lord spoke to her and said she must go and preach the gospel in Asia, Africa, and England. She leads Iris Global which is a Christian humanitarian organization. Her organization is well known for its miracle report across the world. Furthermore, she is a well- established missionary and itinerant preacher who operates in the healing ministry.

After Heidi got married to her husband Rolland, who shared the same vision to reach lost souls, they lived in Asia and England where they always went to the slum of those countries and minister to the drug addicts, prostitutes and the poor. However, years later they wanted to fulfill their call to Africa to preach the gospel through a revival among the poor. They were drawn to Mozambique because it was one of the poorest and most challenging countries in the world. In 1995 the Bakers shifted gear and started to focus on the care of orphans and abandoned children. A year later, Baker became sick with tuberculosis and pneumonia. Despite doctor's orders, she went to a healing meeting in Toronto Canada. There, she had a vision where Jesus showed her thousands of children to feed; when she exclaimed that it was impossible to help them all, he said: "There will always be enough because I died." After which, she was healed.

Since that time, it has been reported that 100 percent of the deaf in the Chiure area have been healed through prayer (Stafford). Scores of others have been raised from the dead, food has been supernaturally multiplied to feed the hungry, the crippled and blind have been restored, and the revival has spread like fire through the gospel of Jesus Christ (Stafford). Church association now numbers 10,000 congregations, maybe more. Baker prayed for two blind beggars who wandered into her tent meeting at her base in Pemba, Mozambique. Both men instantly received their sight after Baker wet her fingers with saliva and touched their eyes.

Heidi has been preaching the gospel for more than 30 years. She has planted over 7,000 bush churches, five Bible schools, and 10,000 Iris affiliated churches in more than 20 nations (Grady).

Since that time Iris Global operations have expanded to include well-drilling, free health clinics, village feeding programs, and other humanitarian aids (Baker). She has established 5000 churches in

Mozambique, with a total of over 10,000 Iris-affiliated churches in more than 20 nations (Baker). She is calling for a passionate tribe of believers who will pour out their life for love's sake and bring all children of all age's home to the Father.

OTHERS

There are more notable soul saving women who are trailblazers in their own rights. These include Jan Crouch, Paula White, Margaret Idahosa, Gloria Copeland, Ann Graham Lotz, Taffi Dollar and others. It was not possible to include all their stories in this book but we honor them and thank the Lord for their gift to mankind and to the Body of Christ.

BEWARE OF JEZEBEL OBSTRUCTION

THE HINDRANCES TO WOMEN in ministry extend beyond men, denominations, and organizations. The Jezebel spirit has been a primary strategy of satan to hinder women in ministry. Many women anointed by God have succumbed to the Jezebel spirit. This has damaged their ministry in different ways. As God raised them up, they begin to display a masculine image thereby giving fuel to those who reject their ministry. Some no longer submit or obey their husbands according to the Bible. Others no longer want to submit to a male leader but try to do it alone or only with other women.

The Jezebel spirit is not to be played with or tolerated because it is a principal spirit. This spirit often comes with insecurity, pride and false doctrine. Victims and agents of the Jezebel spirit too often challenge the pulpits of sound ministries. False doctrine is sending many people to hell.

1 Timothy 6:3 *If any man teach otherwise, and consent not to wholesome words, even the words of our Lord Jesus Christ, and to the doctrine which is according to godliness; 4 He is proud, knowing nothing, but doting about questions and strifes of words, whereof cometh envy, strife, railings, evil surmisings, 5 Perverse disputings of men of corrupt minds, and destitute of the truth, supposing that gain is godliness: from such withdraw thyself.*

One mark of a Jezebel spirit is that they love doctrines that tickle the ear and makes the flesh feels good. They don't like rebukes, the use of the blood of Jesus against evil spirits, spiritual warfare, correction and preaching on holiness, sin and the judgment of God. They almost rest everything on faith, love, and grace. Let us walk in Christ's doctrine as stated in Titus 2:1 *But speak thou the things which become sound doctrine: 10 Not purloining, but shewing all good fidelity; that they may adorn the doctrine of God our Saviour in all things. 11 For the grace of God that bringeth salvation hath appeared to all men, 12 Teaching us that, denying ungodliness and worldly lusts, we should live soberly, righteously, and godly, in this present world.* People under the influence of this spirit will say they are leaving a church because there are too much doom and negative preaching. They prefer a lie, and even when they hear the truth, they will not change.

The meaning of Jezebel is 'unexalted and un-husbanded.' The original meaning of Jezebel is Baalazebel, meaning Baal has exalted. In the Greek, the meaning of Jezebel is "false doctrine." In Hebrew Jezebel means "chaste" because this spirit is very seductive and deceptive. Jezebel is the daughter of Ethbaal. Please note that the meaning of Baal is 'master, lord.' Baal is the most important of the Canaanite gods and is the male counterpart to Ashtaroth. This spirit is connected with immorality, Numbers 25:1 *And Israel abode in Shittim, and the people began to commit whoredom with the daughters of Moab. 3 And Israel joined himself unto Baalpeor: and the anger of the Lord was kindled against Israel.* Baal came about as an opposing spirit to God Almighty and was found among the Moabites during Moses' time. Jezebel introduced Baal into Israel 1 Kings 16:31,32 and her daughter, Athaliah introduced Baal into Judah, 2 Kings 11:17-20.

Jezebel followed her idolatry as stated in 1 Kings 16:31 *And it came to pass, as if it had been a light thing for him to walk in the sins of Jeroboam the son of Nebat, that he took to wife Jezebel the daughter of Ethbaal king of the Zidonians, and went and served Baal, and worshipped him. 32 And he reared up an altar for Baal in the house of Baal, which he had built in Samaria. 33 And Ahab made a grove, and Ahab did more to provoke the Lord God of Israel to anger than all the kings of Israel that were before him.*

We must be reminded that situations and behaviors on earth do not just happen but is either led by the Spirit of God or by the devil. In Ephesians 6:11 we read, *"Put on the whole armour of God, that ye may be able to stand against the wiles of the devil. 12 For we wrestle not against flesh and blood, but against principalities, against powers, against the rulers of the darkness of this world, against spiritual wickedness in high places"*. The Jezebel spirit will oppose churches, pastors, prophets and anyone who has an active call of God. It is so domineering, controlling and rebellious that God's people, wives, and husbands must fight against it.

A principality withstood the great man of God Daniel; similarly, the Jezebel spirit stands against women of God today. Daniel 10:12 *Then said he unto me, Fear not, Daniel: for from the first day that thou didst set thine heart to understand and to chasten thyself before thy God, thy words were heard, and I am come for thy words. 13 But the prince of the kingdom of Persia withstood me one and twenty days: but, lo, Michael, one of the chief princes, came to help me; and I remained there with the kings of Persia.* The difference is that women are attacked in at least two ways. Other women who carry the Jezebel spirit attacks them; otherwise, a woman can allow the Jezebel spirit to influence their own lives by operating in this spirit in their homes and their churches. On top of being manipulated by other women, they will use their gifts to manipulate their husband and their church leaders.

Women are generally hindered in the society so the Jezebel spirit must be carefully identified and expelled. It almost always first begins with a faithful and trusted worker who wilted under great pressure in a personal area of failure or weakness. Sometimes a gifted person had the hearing and sympathy of some contrary leadership, and because of the contrary leader's past faithfulness, they bow to the spirit. Others bow because of the conditions in which they were raised from childhood such as a lack of love, some spoilt, or lacking the basics of a stable home. However, the exposing characteristics are almost always connected with or result in: manipulation, slander, separation, divorce, threats, blackmail, undermining leadership subtly, sexual immorality, lack, rebellion, and uncleanness such as adultery, homosexuality, pornography and so on.

A believer generally cannot be possessed by a demon except by witchcraft, uncleanness, fornication, homosexuality, pornography, rebellion and so forth. A believer, however, can be influenced, oppressed, overshadowed and controlled by demonic spirits. Remember to resist the devil as 1 Peter 5:8-9 says, *"Be sober, be vigilant; because your adversary the devil, as a roaring lion, walketh about, seeking whom he may devour: 9 Whom resist stedfast in the faith..."*. Satan has assigned this Jezebel spirit to churches, families, relationships, great men and women of God to destroy them. Demons use the mediums of men, women, things, animals, systems, and territories. Jezebel spirit comes to oppress and possess men and women to use and destroy them.

There are at least three (3) categories of the Jezebel spirit: (1) Domestic (2) Religious (3) Political. Whatever spheres this demonic spirit comes in, let us resist and fight against it so that true and holy women of God can do the work of the Lord.

Women, for us to be effective in our ministry and our homes, we must get rid of a Jezebel spirit from us and around us. Repent of all sins, idolatry, rebellion, pride, vanity, revenge, stubbornness, fornication, witchcraft, wickedness, murder, covetousness, hatred, lies, crookedness, selfishness, false teaching and false prophecy. Ask for prayer from a holy servant of God or a true prophet. Attend a holiness church that is full of the Holy Ghost and has authority over the Jezebel spirit. Change friends and Jezebel association. Renounce and denounce divination and any dark world activity. Keep in prayer and attend church regularly. Let us adhere to what the scriptures says in 2 Chronicles 7:14 *If my people, which are called by my name, shall humble themselves, and pray, and seek my face, and turn...*

WOMEN OF ZION, ARISE!

THERE IS A CALL from the Spirit of God for women to arise and usher in the end time harvest. Some men of God have caught the vision of God to release women into ministry and are working with the Holy Ghost instead of fighting against the will of the Lord.

For years many in the Body of Christ tried to silence women. In the evidence of many scriptures, no one should try to hinder the ministry of women preachers. The Bible prophesied that women must be used in preaching, witnessing, prophesying and in other ministries.

God's intention for women to arise is for maximum impact worldwide. The devil is using men, women, and children to do his work. Why would not God use women and children to save and preserve life? Isaiah 32:9-20 says that the women must rise up or the gathering will not come. All kinds of desolations and troubles will be taking place until the women rise.

We already see the pains and the calamities upon the earth. It is time for women to arise and reap the harvest. Too long the women are sitting down and being at ease in the kingdom of God. Some have bowed to the misinterpretation of scriptures. Some have erred even when they can find sufficient scriptures proving that women are called to be effective preachers. I pray that the submissive and humble women who are obedient to the Master arise and preach the gospel.

Indeed, when the Bible says to arise, it is not speaking about praying. Many have been praying a lot, and we have also received the outpouring of the Spirit from on high. Now, we see what the problem in the body of Christ is. The women are sitting down, being at ease. O yes, this is the problem. We are armed and ready with prayer and the Holy Ghost and not to preach the gospel.

Are the women different from the men who received the Holy Ghost in Acts of the Apostles and began to speak in tongues and prophesy? Are the women who received the Holy Ghost not to be witnesses locally and all over the world? Like Paul in Acts 16, many thought it could only be men, so they received a vision of a man, and when they look it's a woman (Lydia) doing the job. Women let us arise for the revival at the command of the Lord God Almighty.

Women, because of the troubles and calamities around we must cry out to God until the Spirit be poured upon us. Like the day of Pentecost when they received the baptism of the Holy Ghost they spoke in tongues and prophesied. Women, it is to prophesy the coming of the Lord Jesus. It's time to arise with the Spirit of God and gather souls for the end time revival.

The Bible said in 1 Timothy 2:11-13 that a woman should not usurp authority over her husband. The Bible did not say that women couldn't preach or pastor. It said over "the man" not men. This is showing submission to her husband. The Bible gives guidelines to men, women and young people as to how to live. A guideline as to how to treat your partner does not mean one cannot preach. Anyway, one misunderstood point cannot override the many other scriptures, prophecies, and examples in the Bible.

God is pouring out His spirit on all flesh in the last days. It is not too hard to comprehend the word all. All flesh includes women. Let us not try to twist and to turn the word of God to accommodate our doctrines. Let us again look at Joel 2:28 *And it shall come to pass afterward, that I will pour out my spirit upon all flesh; and your sons and your daughters shall prophesy, your old men shall dream dreams, your young men shall see visions: 29 And also upon the servants and upon the handmaids in those days will I pour out my spirit.* This scripture passage is again repeated in Acts 2:16-21.

According to Joel 2:28, God said He would pour out His Spirit upon all flesh, on the sons as well as on the daughters. The Bible went on to tell us that the daughters will also prophesy. The meaning of prophecy is to proclaim by inspiration, the will of God. A prophet is an inspired messenger who declares the will of God. A prophetess is a female prophet. If a woman can proclaim the will of God or prophesy, why can't a woman preach, teach or pastor a church? Was the prophetess Deborah usurping authority over the man because she was a judge and prophesied? No, she did not usurp authority over the man but humbly did her ministry. Deborah would not be known as a godly prophetess if she usurped authority.

Undeniably, women were present during the upper room experience and received the baptism of the Holy Ghost as well. Acts 1:14 *These all continued with one accord in prayer and supplication, with the women, and Mary the mother of Jesus, and with his brethren.*

Women and men received the Holy Ghost to be witnesses. There are no silent witnesses. Acts 1:8 *But ye shall receive power, after that the Holy Ghost is come upon you: and ye shall be witnesses unto me both in Jerusalem, and in all Judaea, and in Samaria, and unto the uttermost part of the earth.*

WHY SHOULD WOMEN RISE UP?

Spirit Baptism: Women are baptized with the Holy Ghost too. Acts 1:8 says *"But ye shall receive power, after that the Holy Ghost is come upon you: and ye shall be witnesses unto me both in Jerusalem, and in all Judaea, and in Samaria, and unto the uttermost part of the earth."* We are not powerless. Women have received the Holy Ghost and will rise up and preach the gospel locally and globally. The Holy Ghost is moving us not to hold our peace but to proclaim the good news.

Women were also there at the day of Pentecost. Acts 1:13 *And when they were come in, they went up into an upper room, where abode both Peter, and James, and John, and Andrew, Philip, and Thomas, Bartholomew, and Matthew, James the son of Alphaeus, and Simon Zelotes, and Judas the brother of James. 14 These all continued with one accord in prayer and supplication, with the women, and Mary the mother of Jesus, and with his brethren".* They were all, including the women, filled with the Holy Ghost as Acts 2:3 says *"And there appeared unto them cloven tongues like as of fire, and it sat upon each of them. 4 And they were all filled with the Holy Ghost, and began to speak with other tongues, as the Spirit gave them utterance."* The women also received power to preach.

Jesus' Automatic Impact on a Woman: Jesus went to the well not only to save the Samaritan woman but also to give her the living water that would flow out of her as John 4:14 *But whosoever drinketh of the water that I shall give him shall never thirst; but the water that I shall give him shall be in him a well of water springing up into everlasting life. 15 The woman saith unto him, Sir, give me this water, that I thirst not, neither come hither to draw.* When we truly believed in the Lord, both men and women God will use us to minister to others as John 7:38 says *"He that believeth on me, as the scripture hath said, out of his belly shall flow rivers of living water."* Life must flow from you to others.

The Woman Brought Souls to Jesus: The Samaritan woman then went into the city and told the Samaritans about Jesus and told them to come and see Jesus Christ. The Samaritan woman shared her testimony which was believed by many and led them to Jesus as John 4:39 says *" And many of the Samaritans of that city believed on him for the saying of* *the woman, which testified, He told me all that ever I did."* This woman was not only witnessing but lifting up her voice loud and declared Jesus Christ to the troubled and thirsty city. Many preached their testimonies to declare the mighty works of God. Jesus did not tell her to go sit down and be quiet. They gathered souls for eternal life in heaven as John 4:36 says *"And he that reapeth receiveth wages, and gathereth fruit unto life eternal: that both he that soweth and he that reapeth may rejoice together".* Women should still be carrying souls to Jesus.

The Harvest is Ripe: Many souls are waiting to hear about Jesus Christ as John 4:35 says, *"Say not ye, There are yet four months, and then cometh harvest? behold, I say unto you, Lift up your eyes, and look on the fields; for they are white already to harvest."* Like the woman at the well, she heard about the Messiah but was still ignorant and needed to listen to the truth. If God can use this woman, He can use anybody to gather sinners into the kingdom of God. This woman preached to the men of Samara also to come to the Savior of the world. The men alone cannot reap the harvest. God is wise and needs both genders to gather souls into the kingdom of God.

Time is short: We do not have a long time to reap the harvest. The women must rise and help to win souls before it's too late for many as John 4:35 says *"Say not ye, There are yet four months, and then cometh harvest? behold, I say unto you, Lift up your eyes, and look on the fields; for they are white already to harvest."* Souls are dying without Jesus every day, and it is obvious that the men alone cannot reach them. Jesus explained to the apostles who returned that the fields are white and ready to harvest and they should not wait for four months. Reaping the harvest on time was far more important to Jesus than eating meat.

More Preachers are needed. Many sinners need to be converted and there are not enough preachers as Matthews 9:38 says, *"Then saith he* unto his disciples, *The harvest truly is plenteous, but the labourers are few."* Are you going to argue about who cannot help the dying sinner? Are you going to walk away or tell others to leave the perishing sinner? Are you going to sit down or tell others to sit back and let sinners die and perish in a Christ-less eternity? Preachers are short because every time you go into the harvest field, sinners turn to the Lord. Every time and everywhere a woman rise to preach, souls are rescued or other preachers arise. Joel 1:11 says *"Be ye ashamed, O ye husbandmen; howl, O ye vinedressers, for the wheat and for t*he barley; *because the harvest of the field is perished."* Answer the call.

Many countries and individuals around the world still have not heard the gospel. Ezekiel 22:30 *And I sought for a man among them, that should make up the hedge, and stand in the gap before me for the land, that I should not destroy it: but I found none.*

The Bible says 'All'. God said that He would use all to do His will. Women are included explicitly in scriptures to be used to prophesy and to preach as Joel 2:28 says, *And it shall come to pass afterward, that I will pour out my spirit upon all flesh; and your sons and your daughters shall prophesy, your old men shall dream dreams, your young men shall see visions: 29 And also upon the servants and upon the handmaids in those days will I pour out my spirit.*

Men and women must rise and preach as Acts 8:1 says *"And Saul was consenting unto his death. And at that time there was a great persecution against the church which was at Jerusalem; and they were all scattered abroad throughout the regions of Judaea and Samaria, except the apostles. 4 Therefore they that were scattered abroad went everywhere preaching the word.*

Moses said in Numbers 11:29 *"And Moses said unto him, Enviest thou for my sake? would God that all the Lord's people were prophets, and that the Lord would put his spirit upon them!"* Paul said to the Corinthian church that they could all prophesy; 1 Corinthians 14:31

says *"For ye may all prophesy one by one, that all may learn, and all may be comforted.* From the Old Testament to the New Testament, we have women who prophesied, taught and preached. If women can prophesy, they can also preach.

Fallen Male Clergy: Women must stand up in these last days to help fill the gap of the fallen clergy. Jeremiah 5:5 *I will get me unto the great men, and will speak unto them; for they have known the way of the Lord, and the judgment of their God: but these have altogether broken the yoke, and burst the bonds. 6 Wherefore a lion out of the forest shall slay them, and a wolf of the evenings shall spoil them, a leopard shall watch over their cities: every one that goeth out thence shall be torn in pieces: because their transgressions are many, and their backslidings are increased.*

Women, we must arise because we are saved to serve just like the men. God chooses us, not only men. We are also the light of the world. What we heard from the Lord in secret must be declared. We are not just here to carry physical babies but also spiritual babies. The woman Anna stood up in the sanctuary before men and boldly prophesied when Mary brought Jesus into the temple.

The Bible talks about the lukewarm Laodicean church in the last days in Revelation 3:16, *"So then because thou art lukewarm, and neither cold nor hot, I will spue thee out of my mouth."* To combat this lukewarm spirit in the last days, God sent His prophetic words to all, both men and women to receive the Holy Ghost and be His witnesses. Rise up women of God because of Daniel 11:33 *And they that understand among the people shall instruct many: yet they shall fall by the sword, and by flame, by captivity, and by spoil, many days.* Yes, declare the word of God, Jeremiah 9:12 *Who is the wise man, that may understand this? And who is he to whom the mouth of the Lord hath spoken, that he may declare it, for what the land perisheth and is burned up like a wilderness, that none passeth through?*

Look at these signature biblical prophecies of the ministry of the daughters of Zion: Micah 4:13 *Arise and thresh, O daughter of Zion: for I will make thine horn iron, and I will make thy hoofs brass: and thou shalt beat in pieces many people: and I will consecrate their gain unto the LORD, and their substance unto the Lord of the whole earth.* (Thresh: separating kernels of grain from the husk. Done by: stick, cartwheels or feet of an ox).

1 Corinthians 9:9 *"For it is written in the law of Moses, thou shalt not muzzle the mouth of the ox that treadeth out the corn. Doth God take care for oxen?"* This is talking about the gathering of souls. Women must preach souls into the kingdom of God. Saints of God, arise and reap the harvest. It is harvest time.

Lamentations 2:19 *Arise, cry out in the night: in the beginning of the watches pour out thine heart like water before the face of the Lord: lift up thy hands toward him for the life of thy young children, that faint for hunger in the top of every street."* If we can cry out to the Lord for children who are being destroyed and dying on the street sides, we can preach and gather them in the kingdom of God.

A SPIRITUAL RIOT

Traditions of men have dispossessed the daughters of Zion from their God given role in the war for the souls of men. Many gifted and anointed women of God are ushered into silence, and inaction as the battle rages, with the pendulum of victory seemingly swinging to the adversary of our souls.

The Lord through the Prophet Isaiah, made a clarion call to all women, "Rise up, ye women that are at ease; hear my voice, ye careless daughters; give ear unto my speech". It will take a spiritual riot or uprising from spirit filled women of God, to ensure that the spiritual vintage or the gathering of the harvest of souls are not wasted eternally. The Spirt has already been poured out from on high, to empower and activate saved women into spiritual combat for souls.

In spite of this, the daughters of Zion are still awaiting approval of the traditional draped counterparts to realize the missing link to affect the maximum harvest, and celebrate in victory. The hour has come for a spiritual riot, despite oppositions, and popular opinions.

In Bible times, five daughters of Zelophehad, refused to accept the norms and be disinherited. It was the law that when a man died, his possession would be inherited by his sons. Zelophehad died in the wilderness, and he had no sons, only five daughters. His daughters were overlooked, as the different tribes in Israel were allotted their inheritance. The daughters arose, and approached Moses, the most revered leader in Israel, and solemnly protest the right to their father's inheritance. They demanded possession among the other tribe of men, even though it was not the custom, for inheritance to be passed to daughters. The man, Moses, was wise in his approach to this very unusual encounter and matter, he sought the Lord.

The Lord spoke to Moses, and said, "the daughters of Zelophehad spoke right, give them a possession and their father's inheritance". A new law of inheritance was established in Israel as a result of the daughters refusing to accept the status quo. If the five daughters of this man had done nothing, and just accept things the way they were, nothing would have changed for them, and for the many daughters in the generations ahead of them. They effected a new thing in Israel, daughters were now able to become heiresses. In the same manner, the daughters of Zion in this age, should arise, and adopt the same disposition, by refusing to be disinherited from the call of God upon their lives.

Women must arise, and realize, that they are authorized by God in these last days to preach, and ignite revival just like any man that God has poured out his Spirit upon and used mightily. In this last leg, it can't be just mighty men of God alone. God has released his hidden arsenals that will bruise the head of the serpent.

The last days outpouring of the Holy Spirit upon all flesh, was not upon sons only; the Spirit was poured out upon daughters and handmaids, which clearly demonstrated God's position in this time concerning his work, and the end time harvest. God doesn't waste his outpouring, it is poured out upon the daughters for a purpose, surely not to close their mouths, but to open it, and prophesy.

The worst global pandemic in a century was a litmus test for the body of Christ worldwide. The whole world witnessed for the first time in many centuries, the predominantly male led churches across globe, locked their doors on parishioners for over a year, resorting to online church. This triggered the worst scattering in the body of Christ since Bible times. Tragedy struck many churches as their sole Pastors or leaders died in the pandemic. Covid-19 is dead, and many churches are still locked, despite many wounded souls that are in need of ministry.

If the men have laid down arms, what should the women do? In this time, necessity is laid upon the daughters of Zion, as result, they should not depend on men for approval, they should instead arise like Jael of Biblical times, and get the job done. The woman, Jael, had no choice but to help, when she encountered one of Israel's mighty enemies who had escaped. Jael wisely invited him into her tent, used hospitality to woo him to sleep, and then wounded him to eternity with a hammer and a tent peg nail, giving Israel a huge victory over the enemy. Her daring feat was a fulfillment of prophecy given by a prophetess before the war began, that the enemy would be sold in the hand of a woman.

God has a way to use the most unlikely vessels to accomplish his purpose, that no flesh can glory in his presence. Praise God for the anointed men and what they have accomplished, however, have we ever stopped to reflect on whether God is pleased with just 1.5 billion born again Christians? Or have we ever asked, is this what God wants? Certainly not. An honest response would ignite an inferno of spiritual riot among the most unexpected candidates for world revival, the women, whom men, both great and small, has left behind. It is a compelling argument to make that God has destined the maximum arrival of world revival, by adding to the equation the woman factor. Jael was certainly a factor, that brought about the greatest result, the same holds true today.

Daughters of Zion, midwives of revival, a spiritual riot is necessary, it's now or never. The women arising is not a cancellation of the ministry of men, but it is an enhancement, that together will topple the adversary. It is not a competition, but a combination never seen before, called the 'All Flesh Effect' (Ezekiel 12:23). Men alone, is not all flesh, that's part flesh, and part flesh can't get the job done.

The uprising of women is God's providence, and that, even though hindered at times, cannot be stopped, whether we agree or disagree. In the book of Joel 2.28, it says, "And it shall come to pass afterward, that I will pour out my spirit upon all flesh; .... and your daughters shall prophesy". Prophecy is the greatest gift endowed by the Holy Spirit. It is the silver bullet of revival against the adversary, and God has given it to both men and women for end time revival. Why should the Daughters of Zion be hindered anymore? The Lord has already given his seal of approval to join a 'Church Planting Revolution, and take up the Pastoral mantle, that has been evidently cast away be some men, great and small.

CONCLUSION

UNPRECEDENTED IN WORLD history, women today are engaged in every aspect of the world stage.

We can lead in any field of the world system and even be on the frontlines in a military war. Women are voicing their opinions about whatever they choose. While we don't acquiesce to the gender disorder propagated by the world system, we do recognize that the tradition of men and misunderstanding of scriptures have led segments of the church to silence women.

Therefore, thousands of women have not manifested their calling. How can we stay quiet and be at ease when sin is raging and destroying many? The gospel has been compromised by mighty men who have gone astray, while women in the church are looked down on and ostracized. They are told to be quiet. "...Ye that mention of the Lord, keep not silence" (Isaiah 62:6). We cannot remain silent as our children are being taught another gospel. In this time, young people are leaving the churches at alarming rates. False religions are rising and radicalizing the system - we cannot keep silent. The women of Zion must cry out for their children that are being destroyed, persecuted and murdered.

Give me a burden for souls Lord! A woman once sang this song in front of thousands. While it seemed regular to some as she raised her voice to utter those words; this should be the cry of every woman that calls upon the name of Jesus. It is not about running to revivals and crusades – although it is a good thing. It is not about getting hands laid on or receiving a word – although those things are needed. After we receive the outpouring from God, we must not sit idle. The Bible said, "rise up ye women that are at ease in Zion"(Isaiah 32:9). It is not time to sit and hear buttered words as we dine at the table. It is time to rise from the table of feasting and take up the word of God, your weapon, and war against the fiery darts of the devil.

In these last days God is raising up an army and women are needed to sound the alarm. Preach the gospel, rebuke, and expel the work of devils. We must war against the enemy for he is battling against us. We must fight for the master's purpose; we must heal the sick and raise the dead. The end of it will be the undeniable truth that God has called you out to save the lost. We are in trouble with God if we do not allow women to preach the gospel and to manifest in the body. How can revival come if there is no womb?

Women are the womb of the gospel; they are the carriers of the seed that was promised by God. Despite the influence of the church, if women cannot speak, there will be no revival. To prevent women from preaching is a disservice to the gospel and robbery of the church of God. Like many women throughout the time of Christ and women in modern-day Christianity, the mandate to go and preach the gospel is apparent. It is our God-given right to be representatives of the gospel of Jesus Christ.

Works Cited and Consulted

"Aimee Semple McPherson Biography." *Encyclopedia of World Biography*, www.notablebiographies.com/MaMo/McPherson-Aimee-Semple.html.

Baker, Rolland. "About Us." *Iris Global - Missionary NGO*, www.iris-global.org/about.

Berglund, Taylor. "CBS Praises 'Mom of Pakistan' Marilyn Hickey as She Boldly Proclaims the Gospel in One of the Most Dangerous Nations." *Charisma News*, www.charismanews.com/world/66678-cbs-praises-mom-of-pakistan-marilyn-hickey-as-she-boldly-proclaims-the-gospel-in-one-of-the-most-dangerous-nations.

Brown, James and Patrick, James. "Muslims Love Me." *CBS News*, CBS Interactive, 7 Aug. 2017, www.cbsnews.com/news/muslims-love-me/.

"Bynum, Juanita 1959–." *Contemporary Black Biography*, Encyclopedia.com, 2018, www.encyclopedia.com/people/literature-and-arts/american-literature-biographies/juanita-bynum.

"FAQ." *Marilyn and Sarah About Us - Marilyn Hickey Ministries*, www.marilynandsarah.org/about/faq/.

Coutts, John. "The Booths' American Mentors | Christian History Magazine." *Christian History Institute*, christianhistoryinstitute.org/magazine/article/booths-american-mentors/.

Draper, Electa. "50 Years Later, Orchard Road Christian Center Pastor Still Going Strong." *The Denver Post*, The Denver Post, 31 July 2010, www.denverpost.com/2010/07/31/50-years-later-orchard-road-christian-center-pastor-still-going-strong/.

Duewel, Wesley L. *Revival Fire*. Duel Literature Trust, 2001.

Eusebius of Caesarea. Church History, 340 AD. Retrieved from http://www.documentacatholicaomnia.eu

Georgiou, Jackie. "Getting to Know the Real Joyce Meyer." *Jesus Christ Changed The World - Joy Magazine*, Aug. 2011, www.joymag.co.za/article.php?id=300.

Grady, J Lee. "Heidi Baker's Uncomfortable Message to America." *CBN.com*, www.cbn.com/spirituallife/churchandministry/Charisma_Grady_HeidiBaker.aspx.

Hagberg, Amy Hammond. "Marilyn and Sarah: Covering the Earth with the Word." *Called: The Lifetime Magazine for Female Pastors & Women in Ministry*, vol. 3, no. 1, 2010, pp. 40–45., www.calledmagazine.com.

Howie, Barbara A. "Phoebe Palmer, 1807 - 1874." *The American Religious Experience*, West Virginia University, are.as.wvu.edu/phebe.htm.

Hyatt, Eddie L. "Lucy Farrow: The Forgotten Apostle of Pentecost." *Charisma Magazine*, www.charismamag.com/spirit/revival/19805-lucy-farrow-the-forgotten-apostle-of-pentecost.

Liardon, Roberts. *Kathryn Kuhlman: a Spiritual Biography of God's Miracle Worker*. Whitaker House, 2005.

McGee, Gary E. "Baptism of the Holy Ghost and Fire! The Revival Legacy of Minnie F. Abrams." *Enrichment Journal - Enriching and Equipping Spirit-Filled Ministers*, enrichmentjournal.ag.org/199803/080_baptism_fire.cfm.

McPherson, Aimee Semple. This Is That Personal Experiences, Sermons and Writings of Aimee Semple. Hardpress Publishing, 2012.

Meyer, Joyce. "About Us: What We Do." *Joyce Meyer Ministries*, www.joycemeyer.org/about/what-we-do.

Minot, John C. *Heroines of Modern Religion*. Ed. Warren D. Foster,. . Books for Libraries Pr., 1970 Pages 196 - 221.

Phoebe Worrall Palmer." Encyclopedia of World Biography. . Encyclopedia.com. 11 Jul. 2018 <http://www.encyclopedia.com>.

Schaff, Philip (ed), Nicene and Post-Nicene Fathers, Series I Volume 11,"John XVI. verse 7" Wm B. Eerdmans Publishing Co., 1956, Kindle Edition.

Scot, Mcknight. *"Junia is Not Alone: Breaking Our Silence About Women in the Bible and the Church Today"*. Patheos Press, 2011).

Shaw, Matthew. "Pandita Ramabai: Mother of India - Part Two of Two." *Indiana Apostolic Trumpet*, intrumpet.com/pentecostalhistory/pandita-ramabai-mother-of-india-part-two-of-two/.

Smith, Amanda. "Amanda Smith, 1837-1915. An Autobiography: the Story of the Lord's Dealings with Mrs. Amanda Smith" *Documenting the South*.. www.docsouth.unc.edu/neh/smitham/smith.html.

Smith, Peter. "Forty Years after Death, Kathryn Kuhlman Still Inspires a Small but Steady Flock." *Pittsburgh Post-Gazette*, 14 Feb. 2016, www.post-gazette.com/local/region/2016/02/14/40-years-after-death-Kathryn-Kuhlman-still-inspires-a-small-but-steady-flock/stories/201602140012.

Stafford, Tim. "Miracles in Mozambique: How Mama Heidi Reaches the Abandoned." *Christian History | Learn the History of Christianity & the Church*, Christianity Today, 18 Feb. 2014, www.christianitytoday.com/ct/2012/may/miracles-in-mozambique.html.

Time Staff. "Influential Evangelicals: Joyce Meyer". *The 25 Most Influential Evangelicals in America*. Time Magazine. 7 Feb. 2005.

Warner, Wayne E. "Maria Woodworth-Etter: A Powerful Voice in the Pentecostal Vanguard." *Enrichment Journal - Enriching and Equipping Spirit-Filled Ministers*, The General Council of the Assemblies of God, enrichmentjournal.ag.org/199901/086_woodsworth_etter.cfm.

Woodworth-Etter. *Holy Ghost Sermons*. Harrison House, 1997.

Unapologetically Free: Dr. Juanita Bynum
Sheen Magazine, 25 Feb. 2020,
https://www.sheenmagazine.com/unapologetically-free-dr-juanita-bynum/

All American Speakers
https://www.allamericanspeakers.com/celebritytalentbios/Juanita+Dr. Bynum/400157

Encyclopedia.com
https://www.encyclopedia.com/people/literature-and-arts/
 american-literature-biographies/juanita-bynum

The Remnant
No More Sheets
http://www.theremnant.com/febdex10.html

www.ingramcontent.com/pod-product-compliance
Ingram Content Group UK Ltd.
Pitfield, Milton Keynes, MK11 3LW, UK
UKHW041953230426
12048UKWH00008B/321